THE
BHAGAVAD
GITA

THE
BHAGAVAD
GITA

The Song of God Retold
in Simplified English

THE ESSENTIAL WISDOM LIBRARY

Edward Viljoen

ST. MARTIN'S
ESSENTIALS
New York

www.stmartins.com

Library of Congress Cataloging-in-Publication Data

Names: Viljoen, Edward, author.

Title: The Bhagavad Gita : the song of God retold in simplified English / Edward Viljoen.

Other titles: Bhagavadgåitåa.

Description: First edition. | New York : St. Martin's Essentials, [2019] | Series: The essential wisdom library | Includes bibliographical references.

Identifiers: LCCN 2019001798 | ISBN 9781250204714 (trade pbk.) | ISBN 9781250204721 (ebook)

Subjects: LCSH: Bhagavadgåitåa—Paraphrases, English.

Classification: LCC BL1138.65 .V55 2019 | DDC 294.5/92404521—dc23

LC record available at https://lccn.loc.gov/2019001798

ISBN 978-1-250-20471-4 (trade paperback)
ISBN 978-1-250-20472-1 (ebook)

Our books may be purchased in bulk for promotional, educational, or business use. Please contact your local bookseller or the Macmillan Corporate and Premium Sales Department at 1-800-221-7945, extension 5442, or by email at MacmillanSpecialMarkets@macmillan.com.

First Edition: June 2019

10 9 8 7 6 5 4 3

Contents

A Note About This Book

The Bhagavad Gita: The Song of God Retold in Simplified English is not an ordinary retelling or translation of the original epic but a compressed and summarized version specifically created for the beginner or uninitiated reader. What sets this edition of the Bhagavad Gita apart from other retellings is that it is designed for readers with no prior experience of Hinduism. To make the original work accessible, I have simplified complex ideas and paraphrased content to create something that is akin to a primer for the first-time reader. I intend to create a point of entry to this magnificent Indian classic which, because of its rich cultural and spiritual references, may seem out of reach to some readers. I hope that, once introduced to the beauty of the Bhagavad Gita, you, the reader will feel equipped and compelled to read one of the many complete translations. I have provided recommendations for that next step at the end of the book.

English has complicated spelling and pronunciation rules with many exceptions, making it difficult to predict how a word should be written or said. This is not the case in Sanskrit, the language of the Bhagavad Gita, where diacritical marks make pronunciation clear and uniform. Unfortunately, the same diacritical marks can make reading confusing to English-language readers. So I use mostly English spelling conventions for Sanskrit words. In Sanskrit *Bhagavad Gita* is a single word that would more accurately be transliterated BhagavadGītā, or Bhagavad-Gita, and Lord Krishna's name is Kṛṣṇa, marked with diacritics to show how to pronounce it. I have decided to use the spelling *Krishna* and the title *Bhagavad Gita* because they are already ubiquitous in English publications.

In the chapter "Hindu Spiritual Worldview," I have used both the English spelling as well as the diacratically marked spelling to help introduce the reader to different ways of presenting common Hindu terms.

THE
BHAGAVAD
GITA

Introduction

Let the scriptures tell you what you should and should not do, Arjuna. Know what the right choices are and live up to them. It is simpler than you think. When you, or anyone, is firmly on the road to enlightenment there is no conflict at all between what you do and what the scriptures advise. —Bhagavad Gita 16:24[1]

The Bhagavad Gita takes place at the high point of a feud between two great families. For our purposes, let us say the feud revolves around an inheritance dispute that culminates in a war as the only way to resolve it. When the two great houses face off on the battlefield, the champion of one house, Prince Arjuna, instructs his chariot driver, Lord Krishna, to take them between the two armies before the battle begins so that he can observe what is going on. Prince Arjuna is overwhelmed by the sight of family and loved ones divided on both sides. Overcome with grief, he declares that he will not fight. Imagine, if you will, all action and activity freezing for the next moments as the chariot driver and the prince discuss life, death, duty, and Divinity.

That's the Bhagavad Gita! And it's called *The Song of God* because the chariot driver is the embodiment and personification of God in the form of Lord Krishna. At first, Prince Arjuna does not fully realize who he is talking to, but as he is drawn deeper into the conversation with his chariot driver, he begins to awaken to something wonderful: that he is communing with Divinity itself. The Bhagavad Gita is the account of that conversation as retold to the blind King Dhritarashtra by the sage Sanjaya. On one side of the battlefield are King Dhritarashtra's sons and their army. On the other side, King Dhritarashtra's nephews (his brother's sons) and their army are gathered to claim what they believe is rightfully theirs.

The Bhagavad Gita assumes that its reader is familiar with Hindu culture, religious concepts, and mythological names. And so it uses terms and ideas from the Upanishads and other sacred texts that many Hindus today would instantly recognize. Not only that, multiple names are given to a single character, and objects—such as chariots and weapons—are referred to by their mythological names. All this can make it somewhat difficult for a first-time reader to follow who is talking to whom about what. In *The Bhagavad Gita: The Song of God Retold in Simplified English,* I have stripped from the original text names and terms that may be too unfamiliar for the first-time readers. I have also purposefully omitted some of the more complex philosophical text. I intend to light a fire of inquiry in the reader, who, I hope, will then proceed to learn more by reading one of the many complete translations of the Bhagavad Gita available today. (See Resources at the back of this book for recommendations of translations and commentaries of the Bhagavad Gita.)

Why a Paraphrase?

My study of the Bible, as an adult, began in a small bookstore in Burbank, California. I discovered a series of booklets paraphrasing the books of the Bible, intended to give students a basic overview, a starting point for further biblical study. I took a few of the booklets home and consumed them voraciously. It was exciting because finally I could understand the previously onerous text. The booklets' straightforward language cut through unnecessary bits and got directly to the storyline's essential details. These paraphrased texts were precisely what I needed to open the door to studying the Bible.

Reading the Bible after devouring these paraphrased booklets was an eye-opening experience. I now had a basic framework within which I could more clearly understand the Bible. I became aware, too, of the challenges early translators had in accurately interpreting the poetic biblical language from ancient cultures into modern English. I was more inclined to view the Bible's stories as metaphors offering insight into spiritual life, relationship conflicts, and resolutions. I read the simplified Bible stories about the courage and strength of ordinary people to face their trials, just like we do today, with excitement and understanding.

Without the introduction to the Bible through the paraphrases, I may never have gone on to read so many of the brilliant contemporary and liberal Bible scholars, such as Bishop John Shelby Spong and Marcus Borg. I may never have freed myself to read the stories of the Bible with openness to the life lessons they offered; I may never have had the liberty to abandon what doesn't apply to contemporary life; I may never have accepted that there are parts of the Bible I don't understand; and, more importantly, I may not have had the confidence to contradict that which is inhumane and goes against human rights and dignity.

I have subsequently enjoyed reading Bible scholars who are not hampered by the need to take the Bible as the literal word of God. I feel freed from the weight of all-or-nothing thinking and as such am more open to the profound life lessons of the Bible. Admittedly, I still don't understand all the biblical cultural references, and occasionally I can't make my way through large portions of the text; but I no longer see any reason not to enjoy and learn from what I can. More importantly, though, this new freedom to explore gave me the desire to begin the same journey of discovery with other spiritual texts.

Reading the Bhagavad Gita for the first time as an absolute beginner, I was met with an ocean-wide mystery of cultural references, unfamiliar traditions, and other difficulties that reminded me of my first reading of the Bible. I remembered that my progress with the Bible started with a paraphrase and decided to take steps toward making the Bhagavad Gita more accessible to me and to others, who have little or no knowledge of what it is, by creating a paraphrase of my own.

After a convocation of ministers for my spiritual movement, Centers for Spiritual Living, which took place in Mexico, I enjoyed some vacation days, unwinding on the beach. I used this time to give my attention to my new fascination: paraphrasing the Bhagavad Gita. I sat on a beach towel with four translations of the Bhagavad Gita. I pored through them verse by verse, asking myself, "As a first-time reader with no knowledge of the Hindu faith or the rich history leading up to the events surrounding the story of the Bhagavad Gita, what simplified version of this text would encourage others to read more without overwhelming them?" And so began my work on *The Bhagavad Gita: The Song of God Retold in Simplified English*.

How to Read This Book

This book starts with the least of what you should know about the Bhagavad Gita that will allow you to enjoy it, followed by a summary of the cast of characters. Then we go directly to the paraphrase. I've saved the backstory from the Mahabharata, the larger work in which the Bhagavad Gita is contained, for after the paraphrase. In that section, I'll explain what the Mahabharata is and its relationship to the Bhagavad Gita. The last part of this book explores one of the important themes of the Bhagavad Gita a little more deeply: devotion as a way of life and the question of why a sacred text is presented in the format of what seems to be an instruction manual for war. Finally, there is a chapter on several basic terms from Hinduism to familiarize the reader further with the Hindu spiritual worldview. I have written each chapter to stand alone so that you can pick up reading anywhere in the book. For that reason, there is some duplication in definitions across sections.

Throughout the book, I make references to some of my favorite editions of the Bhagavad Gita. I have, where possible, footnoted the chapter, verse, and version being referred to unless I am paraphrasing. The appendix has a list of helpful resources, editions of the Bhagavad Gita, the Mahabharata, and the Ramayana (another primary text of Hinduism) that are suitable for first-time readers of these complete texts.

I hope that you will forgive the substantial oversimplification in this paraphrase and see it as intended: an invitation to step closer to, and eventually learn more about, one of the world's most beautiful and life-affirming religious texts.

Enjoy your reading.

Making Its Way to the West

Ralph Waldo Emerson wrote that he owed a magnificent day to the Bhagavad Gita, and that reading it was as if some large, serene ancient intelligence had pondered and answered the questions that trouble us. Henry David Thoreau, by way of Emerson, also came to read and love the Bhagavad Gita and called it a stupendous and cosmogonal philosophy that by comparison made our modern literature seem small and insignificant. Thoreau's writing influenced Mohandas Gandhi who had discovered the Bhagavad Gita earlier in England in 1889 by way of an English translation by Sir Edwin Arnold. And then, in September 1893 in Chicago, a young Hindu addressed the World Parliament of Religions and brought the awareness of Hindu scripture, including the Bhagavad Gita, to some seven thousand people in attendance. In his address, Swami Vivekananda said:

The present convention, which is one of the most august assemblies ever held, is in itself a vindication, a declaration to

the world of the wonderful doctrine preached in the Gita: "Who-
soever comes to me, through whatsoever form, I reach him; all men
are struggling through paths which in the end lead to me."

Sectarianism, bigotry, and its horrible descendant, fanati-
cism, have long possessed this beautiful Earth. They have filled
the earth with violence, drenched it often and often with human
blood, destroyed civilization, and sent whole nations to despair.
Had it not been for these horrible demons, human society would
be far more advanced than it is now.

But their time is come; and I fervently hope that the bell that
tolled this morning in honor of this convention may be the death-
knell of all fanaticism, of all persecutions with the sword or with
the pen, and of all uncharitable feelings between persons wend-
ing their way to the same goal.[2]

Whatever the path that brought the Bhagavad Gita to the
West, I'm grateful that it is available to everyone who may now
discover its message about living in this world without unhealthy
attachment to the outcome of their efforts. The pathway to doing
so, the Bhagavad Gita says, is selfless action, devotion to the Lord
of Love, and steadfast spiritual study. These share a common
theme: softening our grip on the desires that bind us and cause
us suffering.

Swami Vivekananda addressed this redirection of attachments
in a speech to students,[3] saying, "Our focus of action is neither
to save humanity nor to engage in social reforms, not to seek
personal gains, but to realize the indwelling Self Itself." That is
the treasure of the Bhagavad Gita, that in reading it we are led
to discover who we truly are, so that when we perform our duty

in this world—whether that is to feed the hungry, protect the vulnerable, speak up for those who cannot speak for themselves, love our neighbors, or raise our children—we do it all with a steady focus on the presence of the indwelling Self, the Lord of Love, within ourselves and within all beings.

—Edward Viljoen
Santa Rosa, California, 2018

What You Should Know About the Bhagavad Gita

Tell me, Sanjaya, what my sons and the sons of Pandu did, when they gathered on the sacred field of Kurukshetra eager for battle? —Bhagavad Gita 1:1[1]

The Basics

The term *Bhagavad Gita* means the "Song of God" and is the title of an ancient and beloved Hindu sacred scripture. It deals with spiritual concepts such as the nature of existence and the spiritual self (or soul), our relationship with Divinity, consciousness, the practice of devotion, and the importance of doing our duty in life. More about these topics will be discussed later.

Originally written in Sanskrit, the Bhagavad Gita has been translated into every major language of the world. There are hundreds of English versions, and it is also available online in various forms and is often accompanied by commentaries such as in *The Bhagavad Gita According to Gandhi*. The Bhagavad Gita has multiple layers of meaning, like the parables of Jesus of

Nazareth, and covers three main themes: duty, the hidden self in all beings, and the omnipresent nature of God; and it does all of this in eighteen short chapters totaling seven hundred verses.

The four principal characters, in order of appearance, of the Bhagavad Gita are:

- **Sanjaya**, the clairvoyant scribe to King Dhritarashtra
- King **Dhritarashtra**, the blind king, head of the Kauravas, one of the two sides in the upcoming battle.
- Prince **Arjuna**, the son of King Pandu, head of the Pandavas, the other side in the upcoming battle
- Lord **Krishna**, Prince Arjuna's chariot driver and, unbeknownst to Prince Arjuna, the embodiment of God

In the next chapter, you'll read an expanded cast of characters with more details about their roles. However, too many details up front can make it difficult to keep straight who is who, especially because in the Bhagavad Gita the same person is often referred to by numerous names. Lord Krishna, for example, is addressed by many different names, including Unfallen Lord, Supreme Person, Origin of All Beings, God of gods, and Ruler of the World. Each name discloses additional information about his nature and reveals Arjuna's growing awareness of the Divinity steering his chariot. For this beginner's guide, I've kept to one name per character, so you can stay clear on who is being referred to and who is speaking.

The Bhagavad Gita is embedded in a much larger work: the epic poem called the Mahabharata. The Mahabharata is part of the folklore of India and a guide to understanding human nature. It chronicles the history and heartbreaking events that led up to a devastating and insolvable family dispute and the war that inevitably followed. The action takes place on a battlefield, known as Kurukshetra, which is north of modern New Delhi. The dialogue inside the Bhagavad Gita takes place immediately before that massive battle, one that lasted about three weeks wherein almost every person died. It was large-scale war and is thought to be based on actual events from between 3000 and 1000 BCE.

In short, the Bhagavad Gita is the conversation that takes place between two people, Lord Krishna and Prince Arjuna, directly before the battle begins. The conversation is observed from a remote location by the clairvoyant Sanjaya and related to King Dhritarashtra.

The Message of the Gita

The Bhagavad Gita is a guide to spiritual self-discovery, with the goal of returning our awareness to the indwelling presence of the Divine. It advises us to pay attention to the integrity of our soul's duty, practice single-mindedness, remain unattached to outcomes, and to do everything as an act of devotion. It guides the seeker to accurately identify what is real and what is unreal—not unreal in the sense that something does not exist, but in the sense that the external world is endlessly changing and impermanent and cannot be a reliable reference for understanding reality or knowing God. Our problem is that we perceive the world through our senses, which inform our thoughts and feelings. Our challenge, then, is to take command of our senses in the same way the five horses drawing Prince Arjuna's chariot must be commanded lest they send the chariot and its passengers to ruin. To let the horses run where they may is like being attached to and driven by unstable forms. Unstable forms lead reliably to unstable experiences. The Bhagavad Gita strives to give us a different and stable reference point for navigating the world, by exploring the nature of permanent reality, God, as the basis for the life of selfless service, devotion, and peace.

The Bhagavad Gita offers three disciplines by which spiritual life can be approached: the path of detached action, the path of devotion, and the path of knowledge. One of the many names for God in Hinduism is Bhagavan, which means the Adorable One. Therefore, the Bhagavad Gita is the song of the Adorable One, giving a hint about the centrality of the path of devotion throughout the text.

Bhagavad Gita's Cast
of Characters

And Arjuna, standing between the two armies, saw fathers and
grandfathers, teachers, uncles, and brothers, sons and grandsons,
in-laws and friends. Seeing his kinsmen established in opposition,
Arjuna was overcome by sorrow. —Bhagavad Gita 1:26[1]

Prince Arjuna—Arjuna is one of the Pandu princes, a skilled warrior, and the central figure of the Bhagavad Gita. Prince Arjuna is overwhelmed with grief when he realizes that uncles and cousins are facing off to battle one another. He resolves not to fight because he believes no good can come from the war. His chariot driver, Lord Krishna, responds to Prince Arjuna's grief, and the two friends discuss the nature of action, duty, and spirituality in a conversation that is the Bhagavad Gita.

Lord Krishna—Lord Krishna is Prince Arjuna's chariot driver and adviser. Lord Krishna is a friend to both the Kaurava and Pandava families and therefore refuses to take sides or engage in battle. He offers something to each side: they can choose to have either him or his army. Duryodhana of the Kauravas choses Lord Krishna's army, thinking it would give him an advantage over the Pandavas. Lord Krishna gives himself in service to the Pandavas as chariot driver to Prince Arjuna. According to the war convention of the times, chariot drivers cannot engage in battle. In the role of chariot driver, then, Lord Krishna can keep his commitment to not engage in fighting.

Sanjaya—Sanjaya is an adviser to blind King Dhritarashtra. Sanjaya was granted clairvoyance and clairaudience so that he can remotely perceive what is happening on the battlefield. From his location, he mystically sees and hears everything that takes place and recites it all to the blind King Dhritarashtra.

King Dhritarashtra—Dhritarashtra is the blind king, patriarch of the Kaurava family. Although he was the firstborn in his family, he was never legally enthroned according to custom: his blindness disqualified him from becoming king. Nevertheless, he was the de facto ruler, entrusted with watching over the kingdom until his nephews—the sons and heirs of his brother who was the last qualified king—came of age. King Dhritarashtra had one hundred sons of his own and one daughter. His firstborn son, Duryodhana, believes he is entitled to the throne, and that is the source of the disagreement that leads to the tragic war.

King Pandu—Pandu was king of Hastinapur (in present day a city located north of Delhi) and patriarch of the Pandava family. He retired to the forest because of a complicated matter that is explained in "The Backstory from the Mahabharata." When King Pandu retired, he left the kingdom in his brother's care. Dhritarashtra was to rule in Pandu's place until Pandu's son Yudhishthira became king. The story of how his family was established is fascinating, intertwined with divine intervention, curses, blessings, luck, and bizarre misfortune.

The Kauravas—The Kauravas are King Dhritarashtra's children.

The Pandavas—The Pandavas are King Pandu's children, including Prince Arjuna (one of the central characters of the Bhagavad Gita); Yudhishthira, the firstborn and heir to the throne; Bhima; Nakula; and his twin brother, Sahadeva. Their uncle, Dhritarashtra, was entrusted with keeping the kingdom until the Pandava heir grew up. However, things became complicated when Dhritarashtra's own firstborn, Duryodhana, began plotting to take the throne for himself.

Duryodhana—Duryodhana is King Dhritarashtra's firstborn son, challenger to the throne. Duryodhana is preoccupied with the fame and the military skills of his cousins, the Pandavas. Duryodhana obsessively schemes to get rid of his cousins and take the kingdom for himself.

Bhishma—Bhishma is a respected elder, statesman, and adviser to King Dhritarashtra. As a reward for an earlier act of selfless sacrifice and love toward his father,[2] Bhishma receives the ability to determine when he will die. This makes him a formidable foe since he cannot be killed unless he consents to die. He does eventually die later in the battle at an auspicious moment that he selects for himself.

Bhima—Bhima, Arjuna's brother, is commander of the Pandavas' army. He is immensely strong and kills all one hundred of King Dhritarashtra's sons in the battle depicted in the Mahabharata.

Drona—Drona is a master military instructor who taught all the royal princes on both sides of the family. His excellent training ensures that both armies are matched in skill.

The Bhagavad Gita

[A PARAPHRASE]

Chapter One

The blind King Dhritarashtra: Tell me, Sanjaya, what is happening on the field called Kurukshetra where my family, the Kauravas, and my brother's family, the Pandavas are gathered to fight?

Sanjaya, minister to the king: Prince Duryodhana, your eldest son, spoke to his teacher, Drona, saying, "Look at all these famous people assembled for battle. Our army is unlimited in size and commanded by the legendary warrior, our granduncle, Bhishma. The enemy's army is small and is commanded by one of the Pandava brothers, Bhima. In their army is my cousin Prince Arjuna with his chariot driver, Lord Krishna."

And this is what Arjuna said to his chariot driver:

Arjuna: O Lord Krishna, drive my chariot between the two armies. I want to see who is there.

Sanjaya: Then Lord Krishna drove the magnificent chariot between the two armies and said, "Look, Arjuna, here they all are gathered for the battle." Then Arjuna said:

Arjuna: How can I fight these great people? It doesn't make any sense. They are blood relatives and good people. Just thinking about it weakens my resolve. It makes my mouth dry up and gives me the shakes. Even my hair stands on end. I can't believe any good will come of this war. I will not do it.

Sanjaya: Then Arjuna, overwhelmed by grief, threw aside his bow and arrow, fell silent, and sat back in his chariot. Lord Krishna smiled and said to the prince:

Chapter Two

Lord Krishna: You speak sincerely, Prince Arjuna, but your sorrow has no cause. The wise grieve neither for the living nor the dead. There has never been a time when you and I, or any of these people on the battlefield, have not existed. And there will never be a time when we stop existing.

The spirit, your real Self, cannot be punctured by weapons, and fire cannot burn it. Water does not wet it, and the wind cannot dry it. It is infinite, everlasting, and invisible. Knowing this, you should not grieve.

But even if you believed that your spirit, your Self, could die, why would you grieve? After all, death is as inevitable as birth. Since it is unavoidable, why get upset? Just do what is yours to do. Act! If you do not participate in this battle, you would be violating your dharma,[1] which is your purpose for being.

To those people who lack the resolution to do what is before them, the decisions of life are complicated and difficult to make. However, when you overcome the confusion of the physical world, you will become aware of your of unity with all life, and peace and clarity will follow.

Arjuna: I would like to know about people who have attained that kind of peace. I want to know how they live and speak. What are they like?

Lord Krishna: These people are not agitated by grief, nor by lust or fear. They are meditators, and they are able to view good fortune and bad fortune equally. Even though they live in the world—and enjoy living in the world—they are not overpowered by it. They are not overwhelmed by their senses, which crave certain things and specific experiences. They know how to step back and observe life as it happens.

Arjuna, you already know what happens when you think of something over and over again. You become attached to that thing. And when you are attached to a thing, you begin to want to possess it. And when you can't get what you desire, anger and frustration rise, and these cloud your judgment. To step back from these influences and achieve peace requires committed daily spiritual practice.

Chapter Three

Arjuna: You are confusing me, and you seem to be suggesting contradictory things. On the one hand, you say meditation and study are the way to go; yet, on the other hand, you say that I should go ahead and fight. If you consider knowledge to be better than action, why do you want me to engage in this horrible war? What must I do to achieve peace? Can you please give me a straight answer?

Lord Krishna: At the beginning of time, I announced two pathways to this inner peace: the path of contemplation[2] (right thought) and the path of selfless service[3] (right action).

However, it is not possible for any creature to stop being active. All beings act according to their nature. It is a selfish action that causes all the troubles of the world, so I am recommending that you act selflessly, which means without any thought of personal gain.

Selfless action leads to peace because it is born from God. Do your work with the welfare of others always in mind. Not only will it lead to peace, but it will inspire countless others to do the same.

As for me, not even I can stop acting. If I did, creation would end, and everything would cease to exist. Oh, and another thing to keep in mind is that you are not the doer of any action anyway. Instead, you are the knower or the witness. As a result of your knowing, all actions are performed through a subtle interaction of forces. When you think it is you who is doing something, that is when you get attached to how it all works out in the end. Not everyone understands this.

So to simplify, I say, do everything for me, and do it all without any expectations. In this way, you can be sure to escape the complex web of causes and effects, and you can concentrate on doing your duty for me. Discover what is in harmony with your own nature and dedicate yourself to it as a service to me.

Arjuna: What makes us so selfish? It is almost like there is an independent power forcing us to act against our own nature.

Lord Krishna: What seems to be forcing people to act in selfish—even evil—ways is really the accumulation of desires coming together in a robust and irresistible appetite for self-satisfaction.

These desires have their roots in our senses, and sense information can be misleading. Senses are truly powerful. But more potent than senses is the mind. And more powerful than the mind is the will (or your intellect); and that which is above it all is the real Self, the part of you that is not deluded by the information of the sense world.

Chapter Four[4]

Lord Krishna: I told this information to the sun god, Vivasvat,[5] but through the ages, awareness of it has been lost. I'm telling it to you now because I love you so much and because of your devotion to me.

Arjuna: Wait a minute. How could you have told Vivasvat? He lived a long, long time ago, and you were born in more recent time.

Lord Krishna: Ah, but you and I have been through many births. You have forgotten them all, yet I have remembered them all. I remember them because I am changeless and unborn. I am the power in every creature; and through my own primal energy, I (who am infinite) appear in creation in a variety of forms. I do this whenever a decline takes place in the world, so that confidence in the real Self may be reestablished.

When you realize that you are not merely a body and truly become aware of your real Self, you also become aware of your unity in me and cease experiencing yourself as a separate being. By freeing yourself from anger, hate, fear, and attachment, you come to live in the awareness of oneness with me. But ultimately it doesn't matter which path you choose, because all paths lead to unity with me.

For example, some people approach me through sacrifices to gods, others through selfless service. Some live ascetic lives, others give to charity, and yet others take vows. All of these are forms of sacred service, and those who practice them are rewarded by the service itself.

Nevertheless, getting back to our discussion about action and inaction; even very wise people are confused about this, so I'll tell you the secret behind it. To truly understand, you must, first of all, know what action is, what inaction is, and what kind of actions to avoid.

First, here is the mystery. Try to see that there is action in inaction and inaction in action. Or I could say it like this: even when you are doing a thing, something inside you rests. And even when you rest, something inside you is active.

If you understand this, everything you do will be done with complete awareness of the peace at the center. Then your security will not depend on the results of your actions but on what you know to be true. When you are free from expectations and any sense of being able to possess anything or anyone, nothing you do will result in evil of any kind.

Nothing in this world purifies like spiritual wisdom. It can guide us through doubts and selfishness to perfect freedom. No matter if you are the greatest of sinners, this awareness will help you. So, Arjuna, cut through the doubt in your own heart with this wisdom. Get up and walk into that which is before you to do.

Chapter Five

Arjuna: O Lord Krishna, Lord, you are talking in paradoxes. You recommend two paths. On the one hand, you recommend the path of selfless action; and on the other hand, you recommend renunciation of all action. Tell me plainly now, which is better?

Lord Krishna: Each has its merit, and both lead to the same goal. But the path of selfless service is better. The wise see no difference between the renunciation of selfish activities and the performance of one's duties without attachment to the result. They are the same. So whoever is genuinely practicing one path will receive the benefits of both paths. The goal is the same for both.

Those who commit to selfless service find the Self in all creatures, and they remain untouched by any service they perform. They remain aware that they are not the doers. Even when they see, hear, touch, smell, eat, sleep, or move about, they understand all of this to be the action of the senses. If, on the other hand, someone thinks that they are the doer of all these things, they become entangled in what they are doing, always hoping for a specific outcome. But those who are aware see the same Self in a beggar that is in a king, a cow, or an elephant. They are not excited by good fortune and not depressed by bad fortune, because they no longer depend on the things of the world for their happiness.

Through their practice of meditation, they focus attention on spiritual awareness and discover me as the peace at the center of all things.

Chapter Six

Lord Krishna: Those who want to experience this state of unity can do so through meditation. In an appropriately clean and quiet place, they sit straight and keep their eye movement to a minimum. Then they keep their mind focused on the Absolute that underlies all. They hold the senses quiet and do not allow thoughts to wander.

Several things make it difficult to achieve success in meditation. For example, eating too much or too little will interfere with your meditation practice. Temperance in all things is a beneficial approach to life that enhances the effect of meditation practice. When mastered, meditation brings stillness to the mind, a stillness in which the Self reveals itself. In this stillness, you will experience such joy that you will want for nothing. Neither burden nor sorrow will disturb you because you will know who you are.

This work must be approached with patience and sustained practice, always bringing the restless mind gently back to a single point.

Arjuna: O Lord Krishna, this inner stillness you describe is utterly beyond me. I don't understand how the mind, which is so very restless, can achieve any lasting peace. Trying to tame the mind seems to me like trying to control which way the wind will blow.

Lord Krishna: Yes, that is true. But it is possible through regular practice. This is a challenging thing to do if you are not accustomed to self-control. The mind becomes a friend to the one who has control over it and an enemy to the one who is controlled by it.

Arjuna: What happens to someone who has faith but not enough self-control? What if they become caught up in the world and abandon the spiritual path? It troubles me to think that such a person is lost.

Lord Krishna: Oh no, Arjuna, my friend, such a person is not lost or destroyed. No one who at least attempts the spiritual path is ever lost. Their efforts preserve them, and after death, they are reborn in conditions and surroundings best adapted to their further development.

The wisdom acquired in the previous life will be reawakened in them so that nothing once gained will ever be lost by death. In this way, those who progress by doing the best they can will achieve more peace than fanatics who follow extremes. Devoting yourself to the all-pervasive Presence is superior to all lesser pursuits. So, Arjuna, let the awareness of my love and life flow through you. Remember me lovingly and with faith and allow your mind to be always absorbed in me.

Chapter Seven

Lord Krishna: Practice so that your mind is on me always, and you will want nothing else. You will experience me in all of creation, and even beyond creation, for I do have a higher nature that is the source of creation, the universe, and of life itself.

I create everything, and everything depends on me and is sustained by me, just like precious gems rely on the thread passing through them to hold them together as a necklace.

I am the moisture in water, the light in the sun, courage in human hearts, and heat in fire. I am life itself. I am the wisdom of the wise, the strength in the strong, and the ever-present urge in everything to harmonize with life. My eternal spirit is in everything I create.

Life is made up of three primary dispositions, all of which come from me. They are sattva (harmony, truth, and goodness), rajas (activity and passion), and tamas (inactivity, indifference, and ignorance).[6] These all come from me, but I am not in them. These dispositions, or qualities, make up all creation. Nevertheless, you must look beyond them to find me. Many people cannot see me through the illusion created by these dispositions; and so to these people, the material world seems to be the only reality.

People worship me for different reasons: some because they are distressed, others because they seek knowledge, and others because they seek success. Whatever the reason, anyone who follows the spiritual path is blessed. Those who see beyond the illusion of this world and find me everywhere and in everything, such people are rare and truly blessed.

The variety of forms in creation distracts some people. These people worship the objects of creation, and they find that which they seek according to their disposition. I bring them together with the object of their faith. Through lack of understanding, some people think I have entered into a particular form, and so they worship that form. They fail to see my true nature. They fail to see that I am beyond birth and death.

I am changeless. I am the past, present, and future, and there is no one who knows me completely. They are blinded by the pairs of opposites, driven by opposing likes and dislikes, and not aware of me in their lives. Yet I remain aware of them always.

There are those who have freed themselves from this illusion. They are no longer driven by opposing likes and dislikes because they know that I am the source of all life.

Chapter Eight

Arjuna: So tell me then, please, about the following matters: What is God (Brahman[7])? What is the nature of the individual soul (*adhyatma*[8])? What is matter (*adhibhuta*[9])? What is spirit (*adhidaiva*[10])? And what is the nature of action? Tell me also about sacrifice and how it is to be offered, and how are wise people aware of you at the hour of their death?

Lord Krishna: I am God (Brahman), the Universal Life out of which all life flows. I am the eternal Spirit in all, which never dies, though the body is temporary and perishes. My action is creation happening all the time, endlessly. And sacrifice is when you honor and acknowledge me as the Lord within you.

Those who remember me at the hour of death come to me, just as whatever occupies the mind at the time of death determines the next reality. So keep your mind on me all the time while you do your duty today on the battlefield.

There is a spiritual path confirmed in the scriptures that applies to the time of death. When death approaches, remember me, the Lord, your Sustainer. Close down the doorways of your senses and direct your mind inwardly to your heart center. Then focus your energy upward toward the head, repeating the sacred syllable Aum,[11] and you will pass on to bliss.

The person who remembers me in this way, and who is attached to nothing else, easily reaches me. Those who reach me will no longer suffer in an existence of separateness and constant rebirth. They never again return to the endless cycle of creation and destruction, for they are aware of the permanent, unmoving, eternal reality of me, the Lord. They come home.

Chapter Nine

Lord Krishna: Arjuna, because of your faith, I will tell you about the mystery of my being. I am in and through the universes, but not limited by anything in them. This is the great and hidden mystery: I bring forth and support all beings, but I am not confined in them. Through the movement of my subtle energies of creation, I produce a multiplicity of forms from the unity of myself, over and over again. Yet this constant creation does not disturb my nature.

Foolish people who do not look beyond the form of things are deluded and empty. But the wise know me to be the eternal origin of all and give their full attention to me. Spiritual wisdom may be attained through study, and those who study will see my presence everywhere. I am also in every kind of ritual, spiritual practice, or offering. I am the Mother-Father-Parent principle of the universe. When seekers seek, I am the one they are seeking. I am the sum of all knowledge. I am life's goal. I am the silent inner witness. I am the beginning, middle, and end. I am the womb and the seed. I am what is, and what is not.[12]

There are those who follow the rules and practices of formal rituals, and others who worship personal gods or angels. All enjoy the rewards that match these things. And everyone is drawn to the object they worship and rewarded by the nature of that object.

Actually, no matter whom they worship, without realizing it they worship me still. If their worship is full of love and faith, I accept it as intended for me. Nevertheless, without knowledge of me, all must return to the cycle of rebirth. Therefore, Prince, whatever you do—whether it is eating, helping, acting, sitting, even suffering—do it as an offering to me. Offer all your work and action to me, and you will be freed.

I see all beings equally, but to those who worship me, I come to life in them. Even if a sinner begins to worship me, I come alive, and quickly his or her soul[13] begins to harmonize with life.

Anyone who takes refuge in me—no matter their birth, race, gender, or station in life—will find peace.

Chapter Ten

Lord Krishna: There is more to this mystery of my being. No one knows my origin, because all have their source in me. All the qualities of being—discrimination, wisdom, understanding, forgiveness, truth, self-control, peace, pleasure, etc.—have their source in me.

Arjuna: You are God. Ancient wisdom says so, and now I experience it directly from you. I realize that you alone know yourself, so I ask that you tell me about you. I want to know everything about you and how you fill creation. Tell me exactly, so I can understand how to meditate. Tell me in detail; I will never tire of hearing it.

Lord Krishna: Okay. I'll tell you about my divinity. But I'll only mention the most glorious aspects; otherwise, I would go on and on and on for eternity.

I am the spirit at the seat of consciousness in all beings. I am the beginning, middle, and end of all things. I am the innermost self.

I am Vishnu, the compassionate sustainer; I am the brightest of heavenly bodies; I am Indra, god of gods; and I am the most prominent mountain, the highest peak.

Wherever strength, beauty, power, and wisdom exist, I am the best of it, and all of it comes from me.

But of what use is it to know all this in such detail? Just remember, it all comes from me. In fact, it all comes from an infinitesimal fragment of myself.

Chapter Eleven

Arjuna: Ah! You're clearing up a lot for me by describing your infinite glory. I genuinely want to see it now. I want to experience you in your real form. Do you think I am strong enough to see it?

Lord Krishna: Here I am! This is me: a million holy forms. Here is the entire cosmos turning in my body. You cannot see this with ordinary eyes, so I give you spiritual vision at this moment so that you can see the glory awaiting you.

Sanjaya: Then Lord Krishna showed himself to the prince as the Absolute. In this form, the many appeared within the one, with infinite faces in a dazzling vision, each seeing in all directions at once, glorious and radiant. And there within the body of God, the variety of forms of creation appeared united as one.

Filled with awe and wonder, the prince bowed his head with palms joined, as if in prayer, and said:

Arjuna: O Lord, I see it all contained within you. Everything. Countless worlds. Millions of eyes, endless forms. I cannot determine the beginning, middle, or end. Your radiance is blinding me. It is even too bright for the spiritual eye with which you have empowered me. You are the Absolute, touching everything. The heavens and the earth, and all space between are filled with you alone. This is a wonderful and terrible sight because it is overwhelming. I am losing courage and want to get away, but there is nowhere to flee, for you are everywhere. Have mercy on me.

I see within you the two armies gathered to fight here, all being consumed by your radiance. And more, you devour all of creation with your terrible brightness. O my God, who are you? What is this that I'm seeing?

Lord Krishna: You are seeing me as the destroyer, the consumer of all. Do you understand, whether you participate or not, I *will* consume everything? So, do your part without fear or withholding.

Sanjaya: Arjuna trembled in fear. With palms joined, he bowed and said:

Arjuna: No wonder you are praised and worshipped with such delight. How could we not do so? Heaven and earth are filled with your glory. You are all that is and all that is yet to be. You are in the visible and the invisible. You are beyond the duality of being and nonbeing. You are the timeless and final home.

You are above me and below me, before me and behind me; your power is beyond measure. I have taken you for granted. Sometimes I treated you as a mere friend because I did not know.

Now I see you as the parent of creation. O Lord Krishna, my Lord. My love for you wells up in me, and I am filled with reverence and worship for you. Forgive me for not seeing you before. I rejoice in seeing you now but at the same time, it terrifies me. Let me see you as God in a form that is not so overwhelming to look at.

Lord Krishna: Out of my love, I showed you this vision of me. No one has ever seen it, and it can't be achieved through study, sacrifice, charity, or ritual. But don't worry, I will change into a more familiar form.

Sanjaya: Having spoken these words, the Lord once again assumed a gentle form as Lord Krishna.

Arjuna: O Lord Krishna, now that I see your gentle form, I am myself again.

Lord Krishna: I know. It is indeed difficult to see what I have shown you. Even the heavenly hosts long to see me in this aspect. But as I said, it cannot be achieved through the study of the scriptures or self-denial or charity. But by unfailing devotion you can know me, see me, and be united with me.

Chapter Twelve

Arjuna: Lord, what is the better way to worship you? Is it better to worship you as God—as I see you now—or as the eternal formless reality that I experienced a moment ago?

Lord Krishna: Definitely by setting your heart on me with unfailing devotion is the better way. But also, those who strive to know me as the formless reality beyond the reach of thought, they also come to me. But that is a more difficult path to follow if you live in a world of physical things. It is difficult for the physical to realize the nonphysical, for the visible to see the invisible.

So I recommend that you quiet your mind and fix your thoughts on me as the best way for you. But if you cannot, then learn to do so through the regular practice of meditation. If you lack the will for such self-discipline, then practice selfless service. And if you cannot do this, then practice being unattached to the results of your action and do everything for me.

Understanding your actions is better than doing something for the sake of doing it or because you must do it. And to have a practice of meditation is even more beneficial than understanding. Better still is giving up your attachment to results because of the immediate peace that follows.

I love those people who are kind and friendly and compassionate. I love those who are selfless, patient, and self-controlled. I love those who are not agitated by the world or agitating to the world, who neither run toward pleasant goals nor away from difficulties but let things come and go as they happen. I love those who are not puffed up when praised, or depressed when blamed or criticized, but who find their harmony in me wherever they go.

Those who seek me as their goal in life, I love them deeply.

Chapter Thirteen

Lord Krishna: And there is more, Arjuna. I will explain something that will help you understand. Think of the body of creation as a *field.* And think of the part of you that is aware of creation as the *knower.* To add to this idea, I am the knower of the field—in you.

Creation, the field itself, consists of the five parts of sense perception: the five elements; the five sense organs; the five organs of action; and the three components of mind, which are the "I" maker, or ego (ahankara); discrimination (buddhi); and reason (manas) as well as all the undifferentiated energy from which these things evolve.

It is in this field, through an interaction of the elements I have mentioned, that desires, aversions, pleasure, and pain arise. The body, the intellect, and the will also rise from this field.

Those who know this are unmoved by pride or deceit. They

are gentle, forgiving, and filled with inner strength. Those who know that they are the knowers are free from selfish entanglement. They are not even attached to possessions or family but are even minded in all things. They enjoy solitude. They do not run with the crowd.

That Self within you is without senses, yet it functions through the senses. It is beyond time and form, completely independent; and it supports all things and enjoys the play of creation. It is indivisible yet appears divided into many parts. It is creator, preserver, and destroyer all at once. It is the object and source of all wisdom.

Both the field and the knower are endless. The knower is the source of every action, but the field is where sensations exist. The knower witnesses it all.

Whoever realizes this relationship, no matter what path they follow, steps out of the cycle of birth and death and is united with me. Some realize it through meditation, others through study, others through selfless service, and yet others through faithful adherence to a teacher.

Whatever path they follow, they realize that everything exists as a result of the interaction of the knower and the known. Knowing this, they no longer make the mistake of believing in death. They see eternal life at the center of all beings. Seeing this, they harm no one. They recognize that the knower, their true self, remains unmoved. It neither acts nor is touched by action, remaining untroubled even though it is in all of life.

Those who see this find peace.

Chapter Fourteen

Lord Krishna: Now let me tell you more about the subtle forces of creation I have been mentioning. These forces make up the womb into which I place the seed from which everything is born. Three dispositions, or qualities, of the material nature bind everything together.

The first quality (sattva) is harmony, truth, and goodness and is the bond to purity, happiness, and wisdom. The second quality (rajas) is energy or passion and is the bond to compulsion and attachment. The third quality (tamas) is indifference and ignorance and is the bond to delusion, sloth, and indolence.

At any time, in anything, one of these three qualities is dominant and establishes the nature or binding of a thing. For example, when harmony, truth, and goodness dominate, wisdom and understanding shine from that person. When passion dominates, that person is driven by a restless desire to satisfy that passion through possession or the experience of getting. When indifference or ignorance is the ruling quality, that person is easily confused.

Those who live in harmony, truth, and goodness evolve upward. Those who live in passion remain stuck in earthly pursuits, staying where they are. Those who live in indifference or ignorance sink further and further into confusion.

Of course, the knower is beyond the three qualities, and, as I said, those who discover the truth of the knower within are not subject to these forces.

Arjuna: Well then, tell me about when a person has transcended the three qualities. What is that person like?

Lord Krishna: They are unmoved by any of this. They remain impartial whether these forces are active or not. They realize that it is these qualities and the subtle forces of creation at work, so they remain unchanged. They are established in inner peace where I dwell, and so they stay unchanged through pleasure and pain, good times and bad times.

Chapter Fifteen

Lord Krishna: Sages describe this worldly life as a sacred tree with branches below and roots above. It is fed by the three qualities and blooms into the sensory world influencing all actions. People cannot see its complete form. Cut down this worldly tree with your detachment and then find the path that does not return to rebirth. Free yourself from pride and ignorance and remain aware of the real Self within. For once you arrive at that radiant home, there is no leaving it again. I send fragments of myself to become the inner Self in all creatures. I enter at conception and depart at death. The ignorant do not see me within, but the wise recognize me as the driving force of their lives and are aware of me at the hour of their death.

There are two classes of being in this world: the impermanent and the permanent. Bodies are impermanent, but the Self within is eternal. And beyond both the impermanent and permanent is the Highest Self. I am that Highest Self, the Ultimate Person. Whoever knows me as such has found wisdom.

Chapter Sixteen[14]

Lord Krishna: My further advice to you is that you discipline yourself to be sincere, truthful, loving, and selfless in your service. Do not get angry, and harm no living creature. Practice compassion and kindness with patience and a forgiving mind. These qualities lead to freedom and peace.

These qualities are natural to you. You are born with them. But those who follow a downward path ignore them. These people, forsaking their divine tendencies, begin to believe that there is no creator, no pattern, no truth, and no cause. They see none of the interplays of spiritual energies, and they deny Spirit as the knower within them. They are driven by the endless need to satisfy their cravings. As a result, they are anxious and scheming. They are hoarders and strugglers, and they can never be satisfied.

Repeating habits of violence, arrogance, and craving, they abuse even my presence within them. The primary doorways to this self-destructive behavior are labeled lust, anger, and greed. So again, I advise you, don't walk through those doors. Look to the scriptures for your guidance and shape your life to them.

Chapter Seventeen

Arjuna: Now wait a minute. What about people who do not follow the scriptures but who still have hearts of faith? What about them?

Lord Krishna: Ah. Every creature has a faith of some kind. Remember the three qualities of sattva (harmony, truth, and goodness); rajas (energy or passion); and tamas (indifference and ignorance)? People have a faith that conforms to whatever quality is dominant in them. Those in whom sattva is strongest, they have faith in God. Those in whom rajas is strongest, they have faith in power. Those in whom tamas is strongest, they have faith in superstition.

Each of these qualities expresses itself through people's attitudes, food preferences, work habits, etc. Truth-filled people tend toward food that is mild, tasty, agreeable, and nourishing. Passion-filled people tend toward salty, bitter, or spicy food. Indifference-governed folk go for overcooked, bland, stale food that has lost its nutritional value.

Similarly, these qualities govern spiritual practices. Truth-centered people have their thought on the purpose of their observance, whereas passion-centered people go for the show and recognition. Indifferent people miss both the form and the spirit of the practice and stumble their way through their practice without understanding what they are doing or why they are doing it.

To practice with a spirit of calmness, gentleness, and purity is truth centered. To practice with the goal of achieving status or admiration is passion centered, and the rewards are transitory in their effect. To practice for the purpose of gaining power over others is indifference centered and is self-deluding.

Similarly, giving because it is right to do so, without thought of return, is true giving. Giving with regrets or in pursuit of some favor is passion giving. Giving without affection or respect is indifferent giving.

Chapter Eighteen

Arjuna: Lord, please explain to me the different ways of re-nunciation.

Lord Krishna: There is the refraining from selfish acts, and there is the refraining from the fruits of actions. It is a subtle distinction, and there is a confusion of teachings regarding what to give up and what not to give up. Most certain is this: it is not right to renounce responsibility. Instead, to fulfill your responsibility while desiring nothing for yourself is the true meaning of renunciation.

It is a mistake to forsake work and spiritual practice by saying you are renouncing action. That is just self-deception.

Indeed, in a way, it is impossible to renounce action while you live in a body. And, by the way, if you are attached to recognition, you will have mixed rewards, some pleasant and others not. But those who renounce attachment to outcome step out of the reach of karmic consequences.

Five elements contribute to every action: the physical body, the acting mind (or ego), various energies (such as the senses and intellect), various ways of performing action, and the divine will (or the consequences of past actions). Those who do not understand the nature of action think of themselves as doing everything.

There are three moving causes for each action. They are the subject, the object, and knowledge of the object. Similarly, there are three components to the accomplishment of any action: the implement, the act, and the agent. And all of it may be understood in terms of the three qualities of sattva, rajas, and tamas.

In the mode of sattva (harmony, truth, and goodness), one sees the single, undivided One in all beings and performs even obligatory duty without likes and dislikes, remaining unattached to the result. In this mode, one is nonegotistic and has resolve and enthusiasm, while being undisturbed by success or failure.

In the mode of rajas (energy or passion), one sees differences among beings and abandons duty merely because it is difficult or because of fear of physical struggle. In this mode, one performs actions with selfish motives and exerts too much effort, being overattached to the outcome; and greed, violence, and extremes of joy and sorrow are common. In the mode of tamas (indifference and ignorance), one is undisciplined, vulgar, stubborn, and deceitful. In this mode, one is easily depressed and prone to procrastination.

There are also three types of understanding and will. Sattva governs the awareness of when to act and when not to act; rajas causes confusion between what is right and wrong; and tamas-governed people tend to become involved in actions that should be avoided.

There are even three kinds of happiness. Pleasure that is ruled by sattva may seem like poison at first but tastes like honey at the end. A mind that is governed by harmony, goodness, and truth is a mind that is at peace with itself. Pleasure from the senses seems like honey at first but is bitter and poisonous at the end. This is pleasure ruled by rajas. Those who are governed by tamas draw their satisfaction from sleep and intoxication. They are deluded both in the beginning and the end.

There is no being, either on earth or among celestial beings, who is free from these three modes.

Let me tell you how, by devotion to your duty, you can attain spiritual perfection. It is better to perform one's duties imperfectly than to master the duties of another. Perform your natural duty to the best of your ability, as a service to the Divine, without the tendency to abandon duties because they are imperfect. Every action, every activity is surrounded by defects. Further, it is essential to purify the mind through spiritual practice and to step back from the influence of the senses with resolve, so that you can avoid being governed by the illusion of likes and dislikes. Take pleasure in solitude; eat lightly; and take command of your mind, speech, and actions. Make every act an offering to me. Remember me in every activity, and you will overcome every difficulty through my grace.

You have been given this wisdom, yet you remain free to do as you choose. But do not share this wisdom with those who lack devotion or self-control.

Here is my promise to you. If anyone reads or studies these teachings that I am giving to you, I will consider that, by doing so, they have worshipped me. Such worship I consider a sacrifice well made, and the devotion of their minds shall rise to me.

Even that person who listens to these teachings with faith and without scorn will have both feet pointed toward me, and during his or her periods of rest will be granted access to the perfect peace.

Have you listened attentively, Prince? What is there to say about your previous state of confusion now?

Arjuna: You have dispelled my fears and doubts. Through your grace, my delusions have been dispelled, and my faith is firm. And so I will act.

Sanjaya: This is the conversation I heard between Lord Krishna and Arjuna. Remembering this holy conversation fills me with awe and wonder. Wherever these words of Lord Krishna and Prince Arjuna are heard, there the Lord and prince are present. And where they are present, prosperity, attainment, happiness, and blessings abound. Of this I am sure.

The Backstory from the Mahabharata

The lord does not partake
of anyone's evil or good conduct;
knowledge is obscured by ignorance,
so people are deluded.
—Bhagavad Gita 5:15[1]

The Bhagavad Gita is a small part of the much greater story of the Mahabharata, an ancient Indian epic poem that tells what happens when hatred, jealousy, and vengeance take control of the human heart. The Mahabharata's drama culminates in a larger-than-life battle between two related royal families, the Pandavas and the Kauravas, who can no longer settle their disagreements through diplomatic means. The heartbreak is multiplied when family members face off on the battlefield; uncles, cousins, friends, and relatives end up divided and fighting one another on opposing sides. The only apparent path through the hatred and distrust, it seems, is for the families to fight it out—and they do—until almost no one is left alive.

How Did It Get to This?

It all starts generations earlier with the descendants of the patriarch King Bharata after whom the Mahabharata is named. Promises are made and broken. Secrets and intrigue influence decisions. Honor and pride are put to the test. The intersection of the scheming of supernatural beings with the hopes and aspirations of ordinary humans creates the backstory to this one moment in time, this battle in Northern India some three thousand years before our common era. I will cover some of the fantastic plot twists later in this chapter in "Twists and Turns and Supernatural Solutions." But for now, here are some key points to help understand the bigger picture of the story.

What You Need to Know About the Mahabharata

It's not easy to summarize the world's longest epic poem that tells the story of the descendants of King Bharata. The Mahabharata is many times longer than the *Iliad* and *Odyssey* combined and is filled with cultural references that may be confusing to the first-time reader. I will present here what I think you need to know to understand the importance and placement of the Bhagavad Gita within the Mahabharata.

As mentioned earlier, the Bhagavad Gita is a pivotal moment that is frozen in time when all surrounding action on the battlefield ceases. Not unlike that moment at a party when your focus shifts to a person who becomes so fascinating that everything else fades into the background and time seems to slow

THE FAMILY TREE OF THE PANDAVA AND KAURAVA FAMILIES

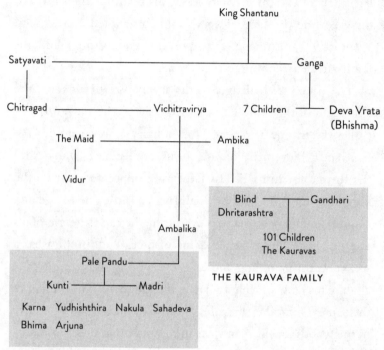

THE KAURAVA FAMILY

THE PANDAVA FAMILY

down. Everything in the Mahabharata that came before, and everything that will come after it, fades into the background while two friends, a prince and a god, discuss the nature of doing one's dharma[2] in life even though every choice seems difficult and unjust. (The paraphrase of this conversation that is the Bhagavad Gita is on page 17.)

Another significant detail about the Mahabharata is that, after generations of conflict, two related families, the Pandavas and the Kauravas, emerge with competing claims to the throne. The oldest son of the Pandavas, Yudhishthira, is the legal heir to the throne. However, his cousins, the Kauravas, disagree; and through trickery, insult, attempted murder, and eventually banishment, they prevent Yudhishthira and his family from ascending to the throne.

The Kaurava challenger to the throne is Duryodhana, the eldest son of the blind King Dhritarashtra who currently occupies the throne as regent. Duryodhana is obsessed with the fame and achievements of his cousins, the Pandavas, and desires the throne for himself. His father was appointed to rule the kingdom until the firstborn Pandava cousin came of age and could rule. Duryodhana tries everything he can to get rid of his cousins, including a rigged game of dice. Yudhishthira has a weakness for gambling and loses everything in the game, including his family's right to live in the kingdom. The winner of the game, Duryodhana, exiles the whole Pandava family to live in the woods for thirteen years in the hope that they won't survive. They do survive, and upon their return at the end of their exile, they discover that their cousins have become accustomed to ruling and are unwilling to surrender the throne. Typically, in the popular retelling of the story of the Mahabharata, attention is given primarily to the events leading up to and during the exile. The adventures of the Pandava family in exile are fabulous and have been retold to generations upon generations of Hindu children as spiritual teaching tools about honor, justice, truthfulness, and the consequences of willfully going against these values. In India, the story has been the source of inspiration for TV shows, movies, and novels. For a full animated movie in

English about the basic storyline, visit the YouTube channel Kids Planet Hindi.[3]

The Only Way to Settle It Is to Fight It Out

After the opposing armies have gathered and are facing off on the battlefield, just before the signal is given for the battle to commence, there is a moment of quiet. Prince Arjuna, one of the Pandava brothers and a hero of the story, asks his chariot driver to take him onto the field between the armies for one last look before all is lost. It is significant that his chariot driver is the Lord Krishna[4] of a neighboring kingdom. Because of his friendships on both sides, Lord Krishna could not engage in the battle but offered a choice to all: either take me or take my massive army. Duryodhana was thrilled to take Lord Krishna's army. In keeping with Duryodhana's greed and aggression, he believed in the power of numbers; whereas the Pandavas choose Lord Krishna, and with him his divine presence and guidance.

At first, it isn't clear to Prince Arjuna who exactly Lord Krishna is, but through their conversation, he soon realizes that Lord Krishna is the embodiment of the Divine. When Prince Arjuna sees friends and family on the opposing side, he becomes dismayed by the potential tragedy of the approaching war and loses his resolve to continue. He can find no way to soothe his feelings of anguish and says that it wouldn't be worth fighting the battle, even if he were to win a kingdom. Dejected, he falls back into his chariot seat and resolves not to fight. Lord Krishna smiles, and what follows between them in this moment of quiet is the conversation that has become known the world over as the Song of God, the Bhagavad Gita, in which Lord Krishna explains the role of personal duty and how it relates to living a spiritual life, the pathways to freedom, and oneness with God.

Next, after an eighteen-day war, the Pandava family wins the battle by destroying the Kaurava forces. It is a devastating ending for both sides. The extensive loss and destruction is a terrible price to pay for bringing matters back into balance, even though the Pandavas rule for thirty-six years after the war.

Twists and Turns and Supernatural Solutions

The Mahabharata explains how everything is connected and how every action is a result of a previous action. Quite a long time before the battle took place on the field of Kurukshetra, forces were at play that set in motion strands of interconnectedness that would eventually bring matters to a head. Throughout the complicated storylines and subplots, the poem emphasizes the relationships between causes and effects, showing how every outcome is linked to something in the near or distant past. It also reveals how the consequence of every action is shaped by the intent behind the choice that causes it.

The story starts generations before the battle, with King Shantanu, a descendant of King Bharata. The two royal families, the Kauravas and the Pandavas, share a common ancestry in King Shantanu. The simplified version of his story, for this beginner's primer, begins when King Shantanu sees a beautiful woman on the banks of a river and falls in love with her. The woman, Ganga, isn't what she appears to be. She is a divine being on a mission of mercy that cannot be interrupted. The couple is so love smitten, that when King Shantanu asks Ganga for her hand in marriage, she agrees on the mysterious condition that he promises never to ask her anything about her personal life and never to question anything that she does. If he breaks the promise, she explains, she will have to leave him.

This seemingly minor event in the Mahabharata reveals a theme that runs throughout: that promises matter. A person is bound by their word; and broken promises lead to consequences like debts that must be paid, now or in the future, by the person who incurred the debt or by their descendants.

King Shantanu promises never to question Ganga. They marry, and Ganga quickly becomes pregnant and gives birth to a son. To everyone's shock and horror she immediately takes her son to the river and drowns him. But because of his promise, the king could not stop her nor question her motives.

Now ordinary people are expected to keep their promises, and sovereigns even more so. The king's word is considered to be law. Breaking his promise is not only a break in personal honor but also a break in the reputation of the kingdom and would set in motion Karmic consequences that would impact the well-being of the whole nation. So the grim reality that faces Shantanu is that he must decide between stopping something quite barbaric, the drowning of a newborn baby, or keeping a promise he made when driven strictly by emotions without consideration of the consequences. The dilemma of making a right decision when strong emotional forces and desires are at play is a central theme throughout the poem and an important teaching of the Bhagavad Gita.

Soon after, Ganga gives birth to another child, who she also drowns, and another, who she drowns. And so it goes, resulting in seven drowned children. When his eighth child is born, the king cannot take it anymore. Not even the bond of his promise or the potentially unfavorable consequences for his nation can prevent him from speaking up and asking Ganga so he can stop what she is apparently about to do.

Ganga is disappointed that Shantanu couldn't keep his word. She reminds him that he has violated his pledge and now she must follow through and leave him to return to her heavenly home. But before she goes, out of affection for him, she tells him the story behind the barbaric and cruel drownings.

It turns out that eight gods, known as Vasus,[5] offended a powerful being, Vasishtha, who cursed them to be incarnated as humans in the world to experience the suffering that humans experience. When the gods heard the curse, seven of them begged for leniency. But the powerful being who had uttered the curse could not go back on his word. He was able only to modify the curse with the service of a celestial being, Ganga, who agreed to temporarily take on human form, give birth to the Vasus, and immediately drown them.

It was a mission of mercy.

The terms of the curse would be fulfilled, but the stay on earth would be shortened by instant drowning. The eighth Vasu, the one who refused to beg, would not be drowned but would live out the terms of the curse on earth as a human.

That eighth child is King Shantanu's son, Devavrata, the sole heir to the throne.

Without Ganga, the king falls into sadness and longing. Some years later, when he is about to retire and turn the kingdom over to Devavrata, the king sees a charming young woman named Satyavati, the daughter of a fisherman. He asks her father for his daughter's hand in marriage. The fisherman is agreeable to the union, with the condition that any child born to Satyavati would ascend to the throne. This creates a complication, because Devavrata and his future offspring are the rightful heirs to the throne. By now the king is sensitive to promises made and the consequences of breaking them. He becomes crestfallen and depressed and returns to his palace. He knows that he can't agree to the fisherman's terms because the throne belongs to his son, Devavrata.

Devavrata's Promise to His Father

When Devavrata finds out what happened, he feels compassion for his father's situation and decides to take matters into his own hands by making a vow of his own. He promises that he will never ascend to the throne, no matter what, and furthermore he promises never to marry so that he won't have any offspring who might challenge the throne at some future point.

In the moment of taking this heroic vow, his name changes from Devavrata to Bhishma, which means "the firm," because of the resoluteness of his decision. For his courage and self-sacrifice, he was granted the power to choose the time of his death, making him a formidable foe on any battlefield.

King Shantanu and Satyavati marry and have two sons, Chitrāngada and Vichitravirya. When the king dies, Satyavati rules the kingdom with Bhishma's guidance, while her children are growing up.

However, things don't work out too well for this family. Both sons die without children, leaving their widows without an heir to the throne. Bhishma and Satyavati send for a famous and powerful sage, Veda Vyasa,[6] to help solve the problem. The sage must be awakened from an intense and long spiritual meditation practice during which he has become gaunt from not eating and somewhat scary to look at. The princess widows are sent to see him one at a time to receive a mantra that will allow them to conceive and produce an heir to the throne. The first found Veda Vyasa so terrifying to look at that she closed her eyes during the moment of conception. The result of her eye shutting is that she gives birth to a blind son, Dhritarashtra, the patriarch of the Kaurava family. The second princess is sent to receive the mantra from Veda Vyasa and is similarly put off by his appearance. Finding him too much to endure she holds her breath during the moment of conception. The result of her breath holding is that she gives birth to a son who is pale and fragile, Pandu, the patriarch of the Pandava family.

Dhritarashtra, although firstborn, because of his blindness is exempted from becoming king, making his brother, the pale Pandu, the heir to the throne.

It seems that things are sorted out when Pandu becomes king and marries two wives. But alas, no. He can't touch his wives, and again the kingdom is in peril of having no successor. Why can't he touch them? One day King Pandu was out hunting and he shot a deer. It turns out that it was a magical being named

Kindama, who had taken on the form of the deer to mate with his partner. Because the magical creature was dying in the act of lovemaking, he cursed King Pandu, saying that the king would die the moment he touched his wives. Smitten with grief, Pandu retires to the forest, leaving his blind brother, Dhritarashtra, on the throne in his absence.

Now one of King Pandu's wives, Kunti, has a secret. Before she was married, she received a mantra that she can use five times to call upon different gods to produce offspring. Secretly, she has already tried it out once calling upon the sun god, Surya, to make sure it works. As a result, she has a son out of wedlock, Karna. She puts the baby in a basket and sends him down the river to fend for himself. It's no wonder that he later turns out to be a bitter and formidable foe against the Pandavas in the battle that surrounds the Bhagavad Gita.

Only four uses of the mantra remain, putting Kunti at risk of being discovered for her illegitimate child. But the princess widows work it out. They call first upon Dharma, the god of righteousness, to produce Yudhishthira the firstborn. Next, they call upon the wind god Vayu, to produce Bhima, the second son; then the chief of gods, Indra, to produce Arjuna, the third son and central character in the Bhagavad Gita; and lastly the twin Ashwin gods, to produce twins, Nakula and Sahadeva, the fourth and fifth children.

Things appear to be sorted out again. But alas they are not. King Pandu, who can't stay away from his wives, touches Madri, only to die in her arms according to the curse of the deer. Madri, devastated that touching her is what killed the king, climbs on the funeral pyre to exit this world with her husband. Kunti heads for the capital to take the boys to King Dhritarashtra so that they can be raised as princes of the kingdom. The sons of Pandu—Yudhishthira, Bhima, Arjuna, Nakula, and Sahadeva—grow up alongside Dhritarashtra's sons, their cousins, the Kauravas.

Surely now things will be stable? Alas, not.

Meet Gandhari

Dhritarashtra guides the kingdom while Pandu's children are growing up. Dhritarashtra marries Gandhari, who has ambitions of her own. After all, her husband is the firstborn in the family, disqualified only because of his blindness. She wonders: Shouldn't her husband's children be the heirs to the throne? In solidarity with her husband, Gandhari blindfolds herself for the rest of her life. She, too, wants to produce children and calls upon the same sage, Veda Vyasa, for his help. While Pandu's wives are working out the use of the mantra to produce children, Gandhari feels the pressure to produce a child first. After all, the firstborn child to a regent—who himself is the firstborn child—should surely be able to lay claim to the throne.

Veda Vyasa tells her it's going to take some time. Gandhari isn't worried about the timing at first, because at that point in the story the Pandava princes have yet to be born. But when Kunti and Madri start producing offspring, things become urgent. After an unusually long pregnancy and some genuinely bizarre complications, Gandhari gives birth to the one hundred sons and one daughter who are known as the Kauravas.

But it's too late. The Pandava princes were born first and therefore are the legal heirs to the kingdom.

The children all grow up together and are trained in the way of courtly life, battle, and spirituality by the same teachers. Uncle Bhishma, seeing the potential for conflict, urges the blind king to name his brother's firstborn, Yudhishthira, as the crown prince and heir to the kingdom. When Duryodhana, eldest of the blind king hears of it, he becomes obsessed with getting rid of his cousins. And so, his scheming begins: he cheats them, tries to burn them while they sleep, humiliates them, and banishes them. All of this leads to the war on the field of Kurukshetra.

The Battle Within

The Mahabharata is more than a story of these episodes of injustices, greed, deceit, and ambition. Woven into the twists and turns are timeless questions about how to live an upright life and how to make the best choices when all options seem bad. More importantly, it is a metaphor for the battles that rage between the competing and conflicting urges in every human mind. Diwaker Ikshit Srivastava, in *Decoding the Metaphor Mahabharata,*[7] observes that dharma,[8] as dealt with in the Mahabharata, is not a set of rigid commandments but principles upon which to live a life of peace and happiness. The Mahabharata offers no easy answers but instead depicts the complex nature of living an authentic life.

The placement of the Bhagavad Gita in the middle of the story is brilliant. It's as if the reader is granted audience to an intensely intimate and private conversation about the very real struggle of how to do what is yours to do without compromising the values that define you. The conversation between Prince Arjuna of the Pandavas and his friend Lord Krishna of a neighboring kingdom is especially beautiful at that moment when Arjuna realizes that he is being instructed by God through this conversation. As a metaphor, it is not unlike those instants in life when during an inner struggle a moment of clarity arises and you see things just as they really are.

Prince Arjuna, like anyone facing an unsolvable dilemma, feels drawn to knowing the truth. He sincerely asks to see the reality of God in full form. Lord Krishna warns him that such a vision into the nature of Divinity is beyond the capabilities of mortal eyes, but Arjuna insists. Because of Lord Krishna's appreciation of Arjuna's earnestness, Krishna grants the prince a look into the nature of the Divine. What Prince Arjuna sees changes him, I imagine, and overwhelms his mortal senses and causes him to plead for a return to a more practical and friendly vision of God that he can relate to. Lord Krishna tells him that no one gets to see him in this form. Though people and gods long to see him in that form, they cannot achieve it by study, rituals, charity, or austerities. Only through single-minded devotion, Lord Krishna says, can a person truly see God.

A Book of War for Times of Peace

Killing these
Must breed but anguish, Krishna! If they be
Guilty, we shall grow guilty by their deaths;
Their sins will light on us, if we shall slay
Those sons of Dhritirashtra, and our kin;
What peace could come of that, O Madhava?[1]
For if indeed, blinded by lust and wrath,
These cannot see, or will not see, the sin
Of kingly lines o'erthrown and kinsmen slain,
How should not we, who see, shun such a crime—
We who perceive the guilt and feel the shame.
—Bhagavad Gita 1:38[2]

Mohandas Gandhi called the Bhagavad Gita a book of priceless worth.[3] He referred to it for guidance and recited certain verses from it as daily prayers. He first encountered the Bhagavad Gita in 1889 when he was twenty years old while studying law in England. Fellow students introduced him to Sir Edwin Arnold's English version of the Bhagavad Gita, *The Song Celestial*. The Bhagavad Gita quickly found its way into Gandhi's heart and became part of the inspiration for his teaching of nonviolence, even though the Bhagavad Gita seems to advocate fighting. Gandhi took the Bhagavad Gita as a metaphor, without denying that a historical battle may have taken place. Gandhi asserted that although the Bhagavad Gita is set at the beginning of a war, and that the opening chapters clearly speak in favor of war, its teachings when practiced lead unquestionably to nonviolence, peace, introspection, honor, devotion, and selfless service. Gandhi read the Bhagavad Gita in the context of its time when war was a standard method of resolving disagreements. He thought that the idea of war might seem brutal to some today, just as the habit of drinking milk today might seem cruel and barbaric to some in future generations. The question of how to conduct oneself in each age, he believed, must be answered within the norms of that age.

Even though Lord Krishna urges Prince Arjuna to do his duty as a warrior in a time of war, the Bhagavad Gita moves swiftly away from the subject of warfare and offers neither military strategy nor combat advice. Instead, it delves into spiritual ethics, the practice of devotion, and knowledge of the Divine. It is indeed, as Gandhi suggests, difficult to imagine how studying the Bhagavad Gita could lead to violence. How, then, do we reconcile its message of union with the Divine and its placement on the eve of a fierce battle? Eknath Easwaran argues that the Bhagavad Gita is not properly part of the Mahabharata. Instead, he asserts that it was likely inserted into the epic poem, and that its message does not develop the story of war but is somewhat at odds with it.[4] Notably, the outcome of the battle is not happiness but loss and regret. So, if the Bhagavad Gita is to be taken as in favor of war, it is important to consider the heartbreaking outcome: the destruction of almost everyone. In that regard, its message may be thought of as a warning about the tragedy of war.

The battle in the Mahabharata may also be thought of metaphorically as the war taking place within an individual and the Bhagavad Gita as the spiritual manual that—when followed— changes our inclination from struggling with our lower urges to pursuing the highest that is within us. For the modern reader, the question is less about whether to wage war in today's world and more about how to navigate through the competing powers of darkness and light in our own lives. The Bhagavad Gita explains that, when swayed by obsession, greed, or anger, we begin a downward-spiraling journey away from our true nature. It advises us to be disciplined and to turn away from our lower urges, fixing our mind on love and doing what is ours to do as an offering of devotion to the Creator. In this way, rather than as a guide for how to engage in war, the Bhagavad Gita is a manual for developing a peaceful mind by disengaging from unhealthy obsessions and the desire to control life.

We may not be in the habit of physically assaulting others, but war may be waging in our minds where our thoughts are fleeing from fears; wrestling with suspicion, jealousy, and envy; or being tempted by the impulse to retaliate, just like the characters in the Mahabharata. When we become mesmerized by lower thoughts—such as pride, greed, lust, envy, gluttony, wrath, and sloth—we find ourselves harvesting the yield that matches these powerful urges. Suppression of such inner battles can't be accomplished by a strict act of will alone or through self-condemnation. It comes, the Bhagavad Gita says, through yielding to and serving Divinity, dwelling on Divinity, and then acting appropriately.

To accomplish this spiritual approach to life, the Bhagavad Gita emphasizes the importance of managing the mind, which it acknowledges is indeed capricious and difficult to manage. In chapter four, verse thirty-four, Arjuna describes the mind as being as impossible to control as the wind. Lord Krishna agrees but assures him that it can be done. He says that inner turmoil ceases for the one who has appropriately controlled their thoughts, reactions, and compulsions. The practical instructions in the Bhagavad Gita on how to achieve this stability of mind are less detailed than one might expect. Perhaps precise instructions were not deemed to be necessary because the original early reader was already familiar with the practice of sitting in meditation. Lord Krishna's sparse instructions, which I expand upon in my book *The Power of Meditation: An Ancient Technique to Access Your Inner Power,* are to select an appropriately clean and quiet place, sit straight, keep your eyes from wandering by focusing the gaze on the tip of your nose, and become engrossed in the Divine. This practice, Lord Krishna says, will dissolve all fears and integrate all the parts of your being for lasting joy.

And the Bhagavad Gita does issue a stern warning, that failure to address the inner battle of our unruly minds and lowest urges will lead to disastrous results. In a surprisingly harsh tone, a switch from the typical intimacy and warmth throughout, chapter sixteen spells out the danger of succumbing to those negative tendencies that lead us downward and away from our spiritual selves. Perhaps these competing tendencies—

one leading us upward to freedom and the other leading us downward to bondage—are like the warring families of the Mahabharata. One is noble, governed by duty and honor; the other is ruled by competition, power, and is willing to abandon honor to succeed. Two families sharing one origin—in other words, both good and evil from the same source, turning the winner into the loser and vice versa.

As mentioned before, the language in this chapter is sharply different in tone, possibly to emphasize the serious consequences of following our lower impulses. As a remedy, it lists details of the virtues that must be embodied to displace tendencies which, in various editions of the Bhagavad Gita, are described as deadly sins, demonic natures, or the degenerate destiny. Stephen Mitchell, in his notes to the introduction of *Bhagavad Gita: A New Translation,* suggests that chapters thirteen to eighteen do not match the poetry and spirituality of the rest of the Bhagavad Gita and may be a later addition, either written by a different author or for reaching a less spiritually mature audience with practical guidance for self-improvement.

The Bhagavad Gita offers fearlessness, purity of heart, dedication, generosity, truthfulness, and sincerity as the antidotes to hypocrisy, pride, arrogance, and harshness. The three gates, the Bhagavad Gita says, by which we enter self-destructive behaviors are desire, anger, and greed, which, when succumbed to, lead in a progressively intensifying downward spiral to a delusional hell of our own making. The way out of such a degenerate destiny, the Bhagavad Gita advises, is to turn away from desire, anger, and greed; to be firm in spiritual study; to pursue the understanding of what Divinity is; and then to let your choices and actions be guided by that understanding. In other words, freedom comes from giving up trying to manipulate the outcome of the duties you perform in life, not in the sense of being indifferent to what happens but in the sense of putting your trust squarely on the inherent holiness at your center and having faith that serving it will produce peace and right results.

In my opinion, applying the lessons of the Bhagavad Gita cannot lead to war. Yet some people have indeed focused on the instruction to fight in a literal sense. Wendy Doniger, a professor of the history of religions at the University of Chicago, wrote that Gandhi ignored the warrior-encouraging Bhagavad Gita at his peril, because the man who killed him was driven by the Bhagavad Gita. That man was Nathuram Godse, and he shot two bullets at point-blank range, tragically killing Gandhi. Doniger writes, "Two days before his execution, Godse wrote a final letter to his parents in which he argued that 'Lord Krishna, in war and otherwise, killed many a self-opinionated and influential persons for the betterment of the world, and even in the Gita He has time and again counseled Arjuna to kill his near and dear ones and ultimately persuaded him to do so.' Evidently, Godse concluded that Krishna would have wanted him to assassinate the 'influential' Gandhi for the betterment of the world. Like the revolutionary Khudiram Bose,[5] Godse carried a copy of the Gita on the morning of his execution."[6]

The Path of Devotion—Bhakti Yoga

Not agitating the world or by it agitated, they stand above the
sway of elation, competition, and fear: that one is my beloved.
—Bhagavad Gita 12:15[1]

Chapter twelve of the Bhagavad Gita lays out the path of devotion as the way to discover that our deep need is not only to
love and be loved but to be united with Divinity through love.
This chapter is sometimes called "The Way of Divine Love"
or "The Yoga of Devotion" and outlines the importance of
devotional love in living a life of meaning. Elsewhere in the
Bhagavad Gita the paths of service and knowledge are empha-
sized. But here, love is presented as the way to move through
life's struggles to peace. The Bhagavad Gita uses the Sanskrit
phrase *bhakti yoga* to describe a love, or devotion-focused spiritual path to freedom in service to a personal form of God.

At the beginning of chapter twelve, Prince Arjuna asks Lord
Krishna which kind of devotee has the greater understanding
of yoga—those who worship Lord Krishna with steadfast love,
or those who worship him as the unmanifest and changeless?

The question reveals that Arjuna is struggling to find clarity about the best approach. Is loving God enough, or is grappling with the ultimate nature of reality better? Lord Krishna, as the Lord of Love, in his response makes room for every kind of spiritual seeking. He says that for those who set their hearts on him unfailingly, the way of love is sure and swift, while at the same time other paths lead to him, too. Lord Krishna avoids the either-or approach to spiritual progress. He advocates that each person give themselves wholeheartedly to the path they choose. He advises Arjuna to let his mind dwell on God, to still his mind there. That, he says, will, without doubt, result in the Lord of Love dwelling in Arjuna's heart. Lord Krishna elaborates compassionately, saying that if Arjuna can't still his mind, he might want to learn the discipline of meditation and, if that is beyond his reach, to try acts of selfless service. And if that, too, is impossibly difficult, he should go ahead and practice accepting life, just the way that it is and just the way that it is not.

Lord Krishna, speaking as the embodiment of divine love, acknowledges the difficulty of having a loving heart in times when life is a struggle or when we are particularly driven by sensory gratification. It seems he is not willing to agree that such difficulty should be allowed to distract us from the goal of cultivating love as a primary mode of being. He admits that all paths ultimately lead to the same destination of union with Divinity, whether that be the path of studying sacred texts, acts of service or charity, or mental concentration. He adds, however, that it is through unfailing devotion to God that one travels more swiftly along the path to peace. The message of chapter twelve of the Bhagavad Gita may be expressed like this: by attending to our duties in life, with love for God as our motive, we experience freedom and joy.

Lord Krishna explains that all spiritual paths followed sincerely turn the seeker into the kind of person that he loves. The person who is loved by Lord Krishna is beautifully described in chapter twelve of the 1885 verse rendition of the Bhagavad Gita by Edwin Arnold:

Who hateth nought
Of all which lives, living himself benign,
Compassionate, from arrogance exempt,
Exempt from love of self, unchangeable
By good or ill; patient, contented, firm
In faith, mastering himself, true to his word,
Seeking Me, heart and soul; vowed unto Me,—
That man I love!
Who troubleth not his kind,
And is not troubled by them; clear of wrath,
Living too high for gladness, grief, or fear,
That man I love! Who, dwelling quiet-eyed,
Stainless, serene, well-balanced, unperplexed,
Working with Me, yet from all works detached,
That man I love! Who, fixed in faith on Me,
Dotes upon none, scorns none; rejoices not,
And grieves not, letting good or evil hap
Light when it will, and when it will depart,
That man I love! Who, unto friend and foe
Keeping an equal heart, with equal mind
Bears shame and glory; with an equal peace

Takes heat and cold, pleasure and pain; abides
Quit of desires, hears praise or calumny
In passionless restraint, unmoved by each;
Linked by no ties to earth, steadfast in Me,
That man I love! But most of all I love
Those happy ones to whom 'tis life to live
In single fervid faith and love unseeing,
Drinking the blessèd Amrit[2] of my Being!

Where There Is Hatred, Let Me Sow Love

The beautiful prayer of Saint Francis of Assisi is perhaps the closest meditation on the kind of love that Lord Krishna is describing. It focuses the mind more on love as a response to hatred and less on love as something to receive. And yet, the prayer explains that it is inevitable that the one loving will ultimately receive love. I have noticed that when my mind is not loving, I tend to be more rigid about life, deciding how it should be and how people should treat me. When my mind is unloving, my receptivity to the good that is around me is constricted. When I have a more loving attitude, I tend to become less critical about life, people, and events. It is when I am most loving that I tend to be more like the kind of emissary of love that Saint Francis and Lord Krishna describe.

Both the Bhagavad Gita and Saint Francis's prayer set an incredibly high standard for human behavior. To be incapable of ill will and to always return love for hatred seems to be a tall order. Loving the Divine is equally challenging. Lord Krishna says as much by acknowledging that a loving relationship with Absolute Reality is too abstract and out of reach for the average person who lives in a human body. It's difficult to feel warm and connected to a concept such as the infinite or the eternal because humans experience life through their sense perceptions and relate better to tangible reality. So the idea of knowing the infinite and invisible Divinity may indeed seem unattainable. Lord Krishna says there is a way, and I think that it is not unlike the way that is laid out in Saint Francis's prayer: to act without hatred and without seeking consolation or understanding. Speaking as divine love, Lord Krishna says that we are to still our minds in him, to dwell on him, make him the supreme goal of everything we do. This instruction is reminiscent of the commandment in Exodus 20:3, to have no other gods before God. I take these passages from the Bhagavad Gita, the Bible, and Saint Francis's prayer as unified intentions to show us what we are capable of and what we can aspire to as humans on the path of discovering our true nature. The target is indeed set high to inspire us to aim for the best expression of love we can be.

Still Your Mind in Me

I understand the transformative power of dwelling on a quality such as love, whether that be human love or love of the Divine. Meditating on love is a powerful focusing practice, and it changes the way I move through the world. When I dwell on love, love lives in me. Rather than trying to change people or the world, directing my attention to love causes me to have an improved experience of the world. That is because attention is a powerful resource and giving it or withdrawing it affects my awareness. For example, when I don't give my attention to something, it recedes into the background of my awareness. It doesn't disappear, but it becomes less prominent. Or another way of saying this is that when I give my attention to something, it moves into the foreground of my awareness. While it may have been there all along, now I see it clearly. Prince Arjuna starts to see the Lord of Love for what he is when he shifts his focus from grief and despair to the embodiment of the Divine who is driving his chariot. With his mind stilled in the Divine, the prince becomes drawn into the spiritual truth, and his thinking becomes clearer and clearer.

Whether a person stills their mind in Lord Krishna as the Lord of Love, contemplates the prayer of Saint Francis, or merely thinks of the quality of love, the effect is similar: love comes alive and impacts their awareness of life. Whether through neglect or by focusing on something else, it is apparent that when love is the missing ingredient in life, we are disconnected from that essential power that waits for our recognition.

Catherine Ponder, one of America's most prominent teachers of metaphysics wrote: "There are those people who read self-help books and take numerous success courses, who get the idea that mind power is all there is; that if they just use mind power sufficiently, everything will come their way. For a time, they may seem right. They can produce tremendous results through the power of thought and through using its techniques. The time usually comes, though, when they realize that mind power is not enough, and they begin to spin their wheels spiritually."[3]

She explains that their focus is missing an essential element: the heart connection. In a word, love. When that's missing, what's left is effort and effort alone can take them only so far. A mind focused on love is a flowing mind and one that is prone to forgiveness and generosity. Indeed, it is attractive to others. Lord Krishna suggests that when we dwell in love, he, as the Lord of Love, lives in us. He also says that those who neither disturb the world around them nor are disturbed by it are the dearest to him. It may be that the same is true for all of us. Would you rather keep company with someone who has a loving disposition, or with someone who is spiteful? Do you feel more comfortable hanging around someone who tends to forgive quickly, or with someone who is prone to hold grudges? What about people who are generous, or people who are stingy? Whose company do you prefer?

I grew up in a rough neighborhood. The kids there loved to hang out with my grandmother because she genuinely loved them. Although she didn't have an education, wasn't well read, and was strict about behavior and manners, she was caring, kind, generous, and forgiving to the neighborhood kids. For this reason, she had more power to influence them than did their parents. Moreover, she got more obedience and respect from them than even the police officers did. Not only that, even rebellious and dangerous kids would quiet down and listen to her when she spoke.

People will do amazing things for love. When I can't focus

my mind on the Lord of Love as the absolute, unmanifested Supreme Being, I can focus on the kind of love that lived in my grandmother or people like her and then give my attention to bringing it alive in me. I've learned to identify with love when I see it by reminding myself "I am that love" whenever I witness something loving or whenever I read something like the words of Lord Krishna. That's the way I bring love into focus and make it my priority.

It works like magic. Or, more accurately, it works like love. Lord Krishna advises us to still our minds in him so that he will dwell in our hearts. Allegorically, I turn that into daily practice by taking time in the morning to be still before I go out into the world. I may even repeat to myself like a mantra "I am that love" or "I still my mind in love." I might direct it toward friends and family members reciting, "[name] is that love." When I practice in this way, when I dwell on love, it keeps me from falling into bad habits of being too distant with or disconnected from the people around me. When I keep my mind on love, it helps me notice more easily when I'm out of step with my heart. When I feel drawn to resent or criticize someone, I bring the phrase back to the forefront of my awareness, and it changes how I show up.

Bhakti is the path of devotion and has similar expressions in other religions. Bhakti is a form of devotional love that often inspires great art, literature, dance, and music. Bhakti focuses more on selfless service and less on rules and practices. In the Bhagavad Gita, the path of devotion, or bhakti, is presented as superior to all other ways.

The Christian Way of Bhakti

There is a beautiful parallel between the message of the Bhaga-vad Gita and the Christian message of love taught by Jesus of Nazareth and Paul the Apostle. Lord Krishna's instruction in the Bhagavad Gita is to focus attention unswervingly on God and, when working in the world, to do whatever is yours to do as if it were an offering to the Lord of Love. Jesus of Nazareth, in Mark 12:28, answered the question "Of all the command-ments, which is the most important?"[4] by saying it is to love God with all your heart, soul, mind, and strength. He, too, pointed to God as the focus of our entire effort, concentration, and intellect. That is Christian bhakti.

Much in the same way that Hindus might recite portions of the Bhagavad Gita to saturate their awareness with the layers of meaning contained in the sacred verses, a Christian devotional practice may be to meditate on, or think about, the nature of God primarily as revealed in the Christian Scriptures. Medita-tion requires slowing down and intentionally placing our awareness where we want it to be. Lord Krishna acknowledges how difficult it is to control the mind, which moves around like the wind, and recommends that whenever it strays, to bring it back gently to focus entirely on God. The Bhagavad Gita says that a person who practices in this way and maintains awareness of the Divine reaches a state of perfect happiness. Jesus of Naz-areth says that the one who understands that loving God is the most important focus of spiritual life is not far from the king-dom of God.

If one seeks a personal relationship with the Divine, but finds the concept of an ultimate, changeless reality too vague and abstract to develop closeness with, a more personal image of God may be helpful. Bhakti is the practice of directing love to a personal form of God. Underlying the practice of bhakti is the idea that the ultimate expression of God—whether that is Jesus of Nazareth, God the Father, Lord Krishna, or some other form of Divinity—is beyond all names. Bhakti may also be practiced by serving God through loving other people. Jesus followed up on the great commandment to love God with the second important commandment, to love one another. In John 13:34, after washing his student's feet, he gave them a new commandment, to love one another as he had loved them. Indeed, he said that their love for one another would be the outward sign that they were his students or devotees.

Jesus went further, elevating love from ordinary affection to the rigorous and challenging practice of loving when it is extraordinarily difficult to do so. Echoing Lord Krishna's teaching to be equal minded in our response to life's ups and downs, and to treat all beings as if God lived in them, Jesus said to his disciples, "But to you who are listening I say: Love your enemies, do good to those who hate you, bless those who curse you, pray for those who mistreat you" (Luke 6:27–28), and "Bless those who persecute you; bless and do not curse" (Romans 12:14).

The Practice of Love

We follow the path of bhakti yoga[5] by letting go of our attachment to outcomes and making our goal to serve life through loving God. The path of love, bhakti yoga, can be practiced as easily as daily setting aside time to contemplate spiritual teachings, or by silently repeating the name of God, or by thinking of the examples of the great teachers, or by reciting prayers, or by singing praise. Importantly, however, such devotion shouldn't stop when the devotional practice is completed. With sustained practice, the effect of the devotion should start to bleed into the routine tasks of everyday life. With practice, the memory or feeling of these devotionals will begin to influence everything you do. This is an essential component of the path of love that the one practicing can be known by outward signs. How we show up in the world will be a testament to what we are devoted to. In other words, as Lord Krishna says, the object of our devotion gives form and function to our lives.

Jesus expressed this by warning his people that "Whoever claims to love God yet hates a brother or sister is a liar. For whoever does not love their brother and sister, whom they have seen, cannot love God, whom they have not seen" (I John 4:20). Tolstoy, in a letter to Gandhi, articulated the challenge of devoting oneself to the path of love as laid down by Jesus. He wrote that in "Christianity the law of love had been more clearly and definitely given than in any other religion, and that its adherents solemnly recognized it. Yet despite this they deemed the use of force to be permissible, and based their lives on violence—so that the life of the Christian nations presents a greater contradiction between what they believe and the principle on which their lives are built."[6] Lord Krishna sets forth an equally high-minded goal for the seeker, describing the perfect person as one who is incapable of ill will; who returns love for hatred, is full of mercy, self-control; and who has placed their heart firmly on God.

Whether these lofty ideals seem unattainable to a seeker, Hindu or Christian, they remain important ideas to aspire to and give us something to aim for that can result in a life that is more in tune with love.

Hindu Spiritual Worldview

Thus, Arjuna, I have taught you
this most secret doctrine; whoever
learns it, is wise, and has done
all that there is to do.
—Bhagavad Gita 15:20[1]

The complexity of the Hindu spiritual worldview, it seems, makes it possible for Hindus to embrace the idea of multiple, simultaneously true paths. Ambiguity, contradiction, and paradox are not seen as faults to avoid but more as mysteries to embrace and explore. It is not atypical for a Hindu to incorporate teachings from other faith traditions into their own practices, without the need to surrender their Hinduism. I recall a visit to a Hindu temple in Bali where temples are characteristically made from the black lava rock that gives them their distinctive look. In this temple, there was a shock of bold red decor to one side. I asked the guide what it was for, and he explained that it was an alcove dedicated to the bodhisattva Kwan Yin. Many of the tourists to that area venerate Kwan Yin, and the local Hindu

Balinese wanted to accommodate their visitors' desire to pray to the deity of their understanding.

Gandhi drew inspiration from Hindu as well as Christian scriptures. In his autobiography he writes that the New Testament, and especially the Sermon on the Mount, went straight to his heart, stating, "I compared it with the Gita. The verses 'But I say unto you, that ye resist not evil: but whosoever shall smite thee on thy right cheek, turn to him the other also. And if any man take away thy coat let him have thy cloak too,' delighted me beyond measure."[2]

Defining Hinduism is as complicated, or more so, than defining Christianity or many other religious traditions because of the number of ways each religion can be practiced. Within Hinduism, there is a substantial diversity of practice and views, making any general characterization extremely difficult and inadequate. The goal of this beginner's primer is not an exhaustive treatment of Hinduism anyway. It is instead a broad-stroke painting to provide a backdrop for understanding some elements of the tradition that occur more commonly among the many ways of being Hindu. To be clear, in Hinduism we may encounter theists, nontheists, agnostics, monotheists, or polytheists, making an agreement about the nature or existence of Divinity a well-debated topic.

Hindus, who agree on the existence of God may fit into the category of polytheism (the belief in many gods) or monotheism (the belief in one god). For some Hindus, the one supreme being, Brahman, the overarching Deity, can be approached through different forms—such as elementals, demigods, and avatars—and through various practices, making certain varieties of Hinduism quite tolerant and inclusive of other faith traditions and therefore its practitioners resilient against conversion. Answering the question why Christianity didn't succeed in converting India, journalist Tony Joseph writes, "Christianity, probably for the first time, came up against a philosophy and culture that did not feel the need to persecute other faiths, did not find the Christian messiah and his teachings either objectionable or exceptional, and therefore, didn't see why anyone should convert either."[3]

One God, Many Names

In 2003 my spiritual community, the Center for Spiritual Living, in Santa Rosa, studied a different religion each month of the year. During August, we focused on Hinduism and decorated the sanctuary with icons from Hinduism as we had done in prior months with icons of other faiths. We selected a statue of Lord Krishna for the focal point. Just when the statue had been placed on the stage, someone asked, "Are you sure that's Lord Krishna?" We realized we didn't know whether we had selected Lord Krishna or even if the statue we installed was Hindu. After a moment of embarrassment and panic about an imminent cultural faux pas, someone said, "Well, if there is one faith in which it wouldn't be a big deal, it's Hinduism." It turned out we had correctly identified Lord Krishna. Nevertheless, the point was well taken. Lord Krishna says as much in the Bhagavad Gita: that it doesn't matter who you worship, because all sincere worship is ultimately intended for him, and he accepts it as such.

Perhaps some Hindus are more open to inclusion of other spiritual ideas because their own faith traditions have been around for so long and already include so many threads of spiritual thought. Hinduism generally acknowledges the authority of both sacred texts and living teachers. As a result, Hinduism is one of the most fluid and diversely practiced religions in the world. Some Hindus worship God as the father, others as the mother. Some approach the Divine through wisdom and others through the form of an avatar or elemental, and so on. To a non-Hindu, it may appear that Hindus worship several gods. Some indeed may; others, however, recognize one supreme power, God, with many names and many paths on which to worship it. Hinduism is, generally, one of the most tolerant faiths, notwithstanding the difficulties and disagreeing factions it has within it, just as all religious movements are likely to have. Perhaps it is because Hinduism is more than just one religion: it is a whole life system of spirituality, more like a culture or discipline than a religion, one that integrates medicine, religion, health, art, dance, and mysticism.

As mentioned earlier in this chapter, despite significant attempts to convert Hindus to Christianity, little progress was made. I can imagine that to a Hindu the story of Jesus of Nazareth, his love for humanity, his being God on earth, his suffering for the redemption of all sin, resonate closely with the many similar characters and stories in their scriptures. Perhaps this openness is what made it possible for Gandhi to take as much inspiration from the New Testament's Sermon on the Mount as he did from the Bhagavad Gita.

Some Important Terms

Here are some important terms from Hinduism. Among Hindus, these are likely to be familiar concepts, but to non-Hindus, these may require some explanation. They are necessary terms that provide a framework within which to explore the Bhagavad Gita and Hinduism in general.

Sanskrit

Sanskrit is an ancient Indian language of Hinduism, the scriptural Vedas, and the classical literature of India including the Bhagavad Gita. Like Latin in Europe, Sanskrit in India was used by the educated classes for literary and religious purposes for thousands of years and exists today primarily in its written form. It is still one of the official languages of India, and there is, apparently, an effort to reestablish Sanskrit today as a spoken language in Mattur, a village in India. The word *Sanskrit* means something similar to "consecrated" or "refined." Sanskrit is revered as a language of the gods, a divinely revealed language.

Pronunciation is very important in Sanskrit as the sound of each word is thought to be connected to a specific energy. Several words in Sanskrit have no direct English equivalent and may need whole English sentences or phrases to explain accurately what they mean. Added to the difficulty of exact-meaning equivalent words in English is the challenge of accurately capturing the meaning and tone of the poetic language in which the Mahabharata, Bhagavad Gita, and Ramayana are written. In the preface to his translation of the Bhagavad Gita, Sir Edwin Arnold wrote: "The Sanskrit original is written in the *Anushtubh* metre, which cannot be successfully reproduced for Western ears. I have therefore cast it into our flexible blank verse, changing into lyrical measures where the text itself similarly breaks." This explains in part why there are so many different translations and different styles of presenting the ancient poetry of the Bhagavad Gita in modern English.

The Vedas

The Vedas are the most ancient Sanskrit scriptures in Hinduism. The Sanskrit word *Veda* means "knowledge." There are four Vedas: Rig Veda, Sama Veda, Yajur Veda, and Atharva Veda. They are considered to be a direct revelation from God. In the Bhagavad Gita, Lord Krishna says in chapters nine and ten that he *is* the Vedas. He refines his statement further by saying that of the four Vedas he is the Sama Veda. The statement appears in a series of verses in which Lord Krishna identifies himself as the best of the best in all things—the highest mountain, the most sacred mantra, the most renowned among spiritual teachers, and so on. He is painting a picture for Prince Arjuna of the manifestation of divine glories using superlatives to help Arjuna's mortal mind embrace the idea of ultimate perfection. Why Krishna identifies the Sama Veda as the best in this series of superlatives is enigmatic, considering that the Rig Veda is the oldest and most authoritative of the Vedas; and the reason for his statement is not explained in the Bhagavad Gita. It is a hint at where Lord Krishna's reasoning is leading. It may be that he identifies the Sama Veda as the best because it is a compilation of hymns of praise. The Sama Veda sets the information in the

Rig Veda to soul-stirring, devotional music. Lord Krishna's identification with the praise songs reveals the Bhagavad Gita's assertion that the path of devotion is the highest spiritual path to follow.

Upanishads

The Upanishads are ancient mystical documents that are found at the end of each of the four Vedas. Collectively, the Upanishads may also be referred to as Vedanta. The Sanskrit word *anta* means "to end," and so *Vedanta* implies "at the end of the Vedas." (This is an example of Sanskrit's extraordinary fluid ability to create complex vocabulary by combining word fragments.) The Upanishads depict the mystical experience of oneness with the source of all being. Among several hundred, there are 108 principal Upanishads. The word *Upanishad* means "sitting down near." It refers to the practice of sitting at the foot of a master to receive a transmission of spiritual knowledge. The Upanishads are sometimes named after ancient sages with whom they are associated and cover a variety of subjects. The Bhagavad Gita, although different in content and format from the Upanishads, is revered by some as having the same spiritual status as an Upanishad, and also referred to as the bible of Hinduism.

Brahman

Brahman is not to be confused with Brahma. Brahma is a member of the Hindu central trinity of gods (Brahma, Vishnu, Shiva), whereas Brahman is the neutral, ultimate reality of being.

Brahman permeates all of creation and is changeless and infinite. Chapter eight of the Bhagavad Gita is sometimes titled "The Yoga of Brahman" or "The Eternal Godhead." The chapter describes Brahman as being all knowing, ageless, and lodged in our hearts. In the individual, Brahman is known as Atman, or the spiritual self within. Lord Krishna, in the Bhagavad Gita, speaks as the embodiment of Brahman and teaches the ways of unifying with Brahman as the path to freedom from suffering. When Lord Krishna reveals his divine form as the Ultimate Reality to Arjuna, the prince is overwhelmed and understandably pleads with Lord Krishna to return to a more relatable version of his divine self. In response, Lord Krishna acknowledges that the path of knowledge of Brahman is difficult and arduous. He recommends the swifter path of devotion. Doing everything in life, without attachment to outcomes, with sincerity in the heart, and as an offering to God, Lord Krishna says, is the path to take when all others seem difficult to navigate. In chapter eight, Lord Krishna advises us to make a habit of practicing meditation and avoid becoming distracted, especially in the hour of our death, so that as we pass from this world, we may be united with the focus of our meditation: Brahman.

Atman

The Atman is the spiritual self, which, when enlightened, is thought to be one with Brahman, the ultimate reality of being. Atman refers to the core of the individual self or personal consciousness. Sometimes *Atman* is translated into English as *soul*. However, there is quite a confusion of meanings in English for the word *soul* making it an imprecise translation of *Atman*. It is the Sanskrit word for essence, self, and breath. Atman also refers to the Universal Self or center of consciousness in all creation. Atman is the power by which our bodies are maintained and by which we function. Atman is different from the ego which is the sense of self-as-I. In Hinduism, that part of mind which makes a separate sense of I is the ahamkara and describes how the ego is created through identification with external objects and attachment to objects and outcomes. The Atman is not swayed by externals. The problem, however, is that it is very difficult to approach life from the awareness of the Atman when the ego (ahamkara) is taking all the attention. When a person is firmly focused on their possessions or status in life, it is difficult for them to let go of their perceived identity. Lord Krishna advises that the ego must be seen for what it is if the correct identification of our self (Atman) is to develop.

In western terms, the phrase *higher self* may be close to what Atman means, as long as that higher self is located within the individual. The existence of Atman is one of the key differences between Hinduism and Buddhism. Buddhism asserts that there is no such permanent individual soul.

Samsara (Saṁsāra)

Samsara is the repeating cycle of birth and death. It is one of the fundamental ideas of Indian religions and is tied to the concept of Karma, the relationship between causes and consequences. Freedom from Karmic consequences cannot be attained by dodging duty or by retreating from life, because even a choice to not respond to life, or to withdraw from life, has its own Karmic consequences. Instead, freedom comes from fulfilling life's duties with the mind fixed on Divinity and without trying to control the outcome of the actions being performed. The Bhagavad Gita says that freedom from the repeated cycle of deaths and births is attained by forsaking the compelling illusions of the external world, understanding our nature and what makes us act, and acting with a mind and heart stilled in God.

Moksha

Moksha is the freedom that comes from escaping the repeated cycle of birth and death. It is achieved, the Bhagavad Gita says, by renunciation, meaning detachment from the urges that seemingly control us. One of the key ways to accomplish this detachment is through a moral and virtuous life (dharma). It is also helpful to understand what forces are at play in us and the world; and through understanding them, we can learn to avoid being governed by them. The Bhagavad Gita describes how these forces influence everything we do, for better or for worse. When we have learned to notice the urges that arise, we become more skilled at observing what is happening in a detached way without the need to follow the urges. In chapter eighteen, sometimes titled "Freedom and Renunciation," or "The Way of Liberation in Renunciation," Lord Krishna says that by loving him, a person comes to know him truly; and when a person knows him truly, they understand his boundless being; and when such a person performs all their activities in Lord Krishna's service, they win eternal life, liberation from rebirth.

Shraddha (Śraddhā)

Shraddha is an important concept in the Bhagavad Gita. It may be thought of as faith, loyalty, or trust. The Bhagavad Gita explains how the ideas and objects we are loyal to capture our attention and shape our experience of life. We are united with whatever we focus on by way of our faith in it. Creation with its variety and splendor is fascinating. Some people get caught in the trap of becoming distracted by the things in the physical world to the point of forgetting what caused everything to be. The Bhagavad Gita describes three kinds of faith: faith driven by ignorance, faith driven by passion, and faith steeped in goodness. These three qualities—ignorance, passion, and goodness—are an important framework in the Bhagavad Gita through which we can understand ourselves and why we do what we do.

Yoga

Yoga is a group of practices that originated in India. The Sanskrit word *Yoga* means "to unite" and describes practices that reveal the union of the mind with the spiritual self. The four branches of yoga of the Vedic tradition are discussed in the Bhagavad Gita: the yoga of knowledge, the yoga of meditation, the yoga of action, the yoga of devotion.

- jnana-yoga—knowledge, will, determination, study
- raja-yoga—meditation, discipline of mind and senses
- karma-yoga—selfless service to others
- bhakti yoga—devotion, identification with the Lord of Love

Other branches of Yoga not mentioned in the Bhagavad Gita include but are not limited to:

- hatha yoga—discipline of the body through postures, (or asanas)
- japa yoga—the practice of repeating sacred sayings, or mantras
- tantra yoga—the pursuit of enlightenment in this lifetime
- yantra yoga—the study of sacred geometric design to expand awareness
- kundalini yoga—the awakening of primal energy systems through a variety of yoga practices

Yuga

A yuga is a period within a cycle of time and has four sequential stages: Satya Yuga, Treta Yuga, Dvapara Yuga, and Kali Yuga. Each yuga has its distinct characteristic; our current one is a Kali Yuga, the darkest of the four ages. It is thought to have started approximately during the time of Lord Krishna's stay on earth and the battle depicted in the Mahabharata.

The four yugas take place within a larger cycle called a mahayuga that lasts 4,320,000 years. There are several mahayugas (1,000) in a larger cycle of time called a kalpa. This is to say that in the Hindu spiritual worldview, time is cyclical, and creation is not a one-time event. Creation doesn't have a fixed starting point; rather it arises out of Divinity in a cyclical and ongoing basis. Creation appears and dissolves. At the end of this period, the created universe reverts to its uncreated form, and the whole cycle starts over.

Maya

Maya refers to the illusory nature of the world that appears before us. The world may be a real experience but is not ultimate reality. The Bhagavad Gita teaches that, on the one hand, only the creative unchanging power of Divinity is real and, on the other hand, that maya is continuously in flux, changing and moving, and hiding or masking the true nature of reality. Maya is characterized by change, opposites, beginnings, and endings. Ultimate reality is characterized by changelessness, oneness, and is uncaused.

Dharma

Dharma is a Sanskrit word that has no single equivalent meaning in English. The word *duty* is commonly used to translate *dharma* and suggests conformity of one's choices to one's personal duty, or character. Even so, the word *duty* is not sufficient to convey everything *dharma* means. It may be thought of as meaning that which holds everything together, or that which supports the essential order of everything. In the Bhagavad Gita Lord Krishna says that it is better for a person to perform their duty (dharma) poorly, rather than flawlessly performing a duty that belongs to someone else.

Adharma is the opposite of dharma, and the word *adharma* describes the path that leads away from what is yours to do. To understand what dharma and adharma mean, think of duty as something much more than the chores associated with your job or with your station in life. It has something to do with the integrity of your being, that when you depart from it, or neglect it, disharmony follows. For an imperfect example consider what happens when two people fall in love. For this instance, let us use a young man and woman who are attracted to each other, date, get married, and conceive a child. In the moment of conception, the two individuals invoke many strands of duty related to the child they are bringing into the world. One might say their dharma becomes to raise that child; they now have parent duty as a permanent identity that cannot be surrendered. If these parents put their personal desires and goals ahead of raising the child, that might be thought of as going against their parent duty, or adharma. They may desire to stay in the bliss of initial romantic attraction that allowed for their coming together to produce new life, but in this hypothetical situation something happens that makes remaining loving and being kind to each other difficult and the couple questions their ability to stay together.

Nevertheless, and no matter the struggle, the parent duty did not go away when their affection for each other faltered. Someone might ask if staying together as a couple in a loveless marriage characterized by contention and stress is damaging to the child. Is it going against parent duty not to provide role models of love, or is parting to create a loving environment in another format the better choice? The couple must ask the question: How now will parent duty be fulfilled? And *that* is the type of struggle of the Bhagavad Gita, and of Prince Arjuna. There is no easy answer, and many lives are connected, and many consequences await the decision. If he doesn't fight, an unjust ruler will ascend to the throne and many lives will be lost. As a metaphor, the dilemma describes the points of choice in our lives where all options are terrible. The instruction is to engage even though difficulties abound. The emphasis, however, is on engagement without hatred or attachment.

Lord Krishna shows no way to abdicate from your duty; and if you do, it will be perilous for you, those around you, and society. Instead, we are to do our duty, even if the path is difficult, by centering our mind in the Divine (Love), detaching from outcomes, not being disturbed by the world and not being a disturbance, and holding no ill will to anyone. I cannot say if staying together or parting ways is best for our hypothetical couple to fulfill their parent duty. The dilemma illustrates how points of choice exist for us all along life's path, and sometimes all the options seem unsatisfying. Then we must choose the path that best keeps the integrity of our being and perform it.

So think of dharma as acting in ways that are in harmony with the order of the spiritual universe, or with right living. The word *dharma* also means "that which holds everything together," so a choice that goes against your dharma may have the effect of unraveling your equilibrium or integrity.

Not only does Hinduism teach these beautiful concepts through philosophy but through story to make the ideas personal and more relatable. For example, Dharma and Adharma appear in Hindu stories as characters with offspring. The progeny of Dharma tend toward the virtues (devotion, courage, and contentment, etc.), whereas the progeny of Adharma tend toward vices (violence, dishonesty, and fear, etc.).

Karma

The word *karma* means "to do," or "action," and it describes the complex interconnection of all life. *Karma* refers to the idea of cause and effect in which intent and outcome are connected. In the Hindu spiritual worldview, there are different kinds of Karma. Karma can be accumulated in the past, including past lives, and Karma is also created in current time. Karma is individual, and it is collective, too. The Bhagavad Gita teaches that we can never abandon acting in life, but we can aspire to let go of attachment to the result of our actions when we focus our attention on doing everything in life for Divinity. Emotional entanglement with action is what causes difficulties to arise, not action in itself. This is how we can change what kind of Karma we are generating, by changing our motives in life and disconnecting from emotional entanglement. In other words, we have some, not all, control over our destiny through our freedom of choice. We cannot escape from acting in life, but we can choose what type of action we will engage in: personally motivated action (or selfish action), duty-related action (characterized by understanding that the soul remains untouched by action), and action inspired by the love of the Divine (selfless service as an offering to God).

The Philosophy of Sankhya (*sāṁkhya*)

Sankhya is a Hindu philosophy known for its enumeration of qualities and innate tendencies. The philosophy of Sankhya appears in the Bhagavad Gita in the explanation of the energies that are actively influencing life. These qualities are innate tendencies and have three dispositions (ignorance, passion, and goodness) that permeate all of life.

There are two main components of the philosophy of Sankhya that Lord Krishna discusses in the Bhagavad Gita: purusha and prakriti, or the Knower and that which is known. Chapter two of the Bhagavad Gita is sometimes titled "Sankhya Yoga." In it, Lord Krishna explains to Prince Arjuna the cause behind his upset. To do so, Lord Krishna must first explain the nature of reality through the philosophy of Sankhya. Lord Krishna defines several complex topics in this chapter, including Divinity as the ultimate reality; the eternal soul, or Atman, that lives in each person; the body as that which houses the soul; the intelligence that discriminates; the sense of "I am"; the mind as governing the senses; the senses themselves; the elements; and the three dispositions or energies that govern all life.

The philosophy of the Bhagavad Gita may be generalized and simplified as the idea that through stilling our minds, becoming aware of our dominant disposition, detaching from the desire to control the outcome, doing our duty while focusing on the Lord of Love within, we attain freedom.

Veda Vyasa

Veda Vyasa is considered to be the author of the Mahabharata. He is also an essential character in the story in his role of securing the line of succession for the royal families when no children had been born. See "The Backstory from the Mahabharata" on page 45 for a summary of his appearance early in the story. He is an important and revered figure among Hindus, considered by some to be an avatar of Vishnu and esteemed for his role in dividing the Vedas into four volumes. According to Hindu tradition, the sage Veda Vyasa dictated the Mahabharata to the god Ganesha who wrote it down. See more information about Ganesha in the section below.

Some Important Deities

The Trinity

The Hindu trinity consists of Brahma the creator; Vishnu, the sustainer; and Shiva, the destroyer, or dissolver. The trinity represents a partnership, or unity, of divine functions: creating the universe, sustaining it, and then dissolving it so that it can start all over again. In Sanskrit, the trinity is referred to as *Trimūrti*, meaning "three forms."

Brahma and Sarasvati (Sarasvatī)

Brahma is the first member of the trinity, and although he is the creator of the universe, there are relatively few temples dedicated to his worship in India. His wife is Sarasvati, the goddess of learning, knowledge, science, and the arts.

Vishnu and Lakshmi (Lakṣmī)

Vishnu represents that aspect of the Divine that maintains and sustains the universe. Vishnu's wife is Lakshmi, goddess of wealth, good fortune, and prosperity. In his role of maintainer of the universe, Vishnu returns to earth from time to time to restore balance when there is a decline in morality among humankind.

Shiva and Parvati

Shiva is the third aspect of God in the trinity. His function is to dissolve the universe so that the next cycle of creation can take place. Shiva's wife is Parvati, the goddess of love and fertility.

Ganesha

Ganesha is easiest to identify among Hindu gods because of the elephant's head on a human body. He is the son of Shiva and Parvati. Hindus appeal to Ganesha at the beginning of important events, like the start of new business, because he is known as the remover of obstacles and the bringer of good fortune, prosperity, and success. He is often depicted with one broken tusk because of his role as the scribe of the Mahabharata. The popular story is that Ganesha broke off his tusk to continue writing the Mahabharata while Veda Vyasa was dictating it. There are, however, other accounts of how he may have lost his tusk.

How Ganesha came to have an elephant's head is also a popular story in Hinduism. His mother, Parvati, was taking a bath and gave Ganesha the task of guarding her privacy. Ganesha and his father, Shiva, hadn't yet met. So, when Shiva appeared after a long absence, eager to see his wife, he was met by a strange young man who prevented him from entering his wife's bath area. In a fit of impatience and anger, he cut the boy's head off. Parvati was furious. Shiva sent his minions to find the head of the first creature they came upon. They returned with an elephant head and quickly affixed it to the boy, bringing him back to life.

Hanuman

Hanuman is another Hindu god better known in the Western world because of his monkey-like appearance. Strictly speaking, he is not a monkey, but a Vanara, a mythological, or supernatural being, that has speech, clothing, culture, and rituals. Hanuman, in the Ramayana, helps Prince Rama retrieve his abducted wife, Princess Sita, by rallying the Vanaras who build a bridge from India to Lanka for Prince Rama to cross.

Hanuman has a small appearance in the Bhagavad Gita, on the emblem of Prince Arjuna's banner. Here he stands as a reminder to the prince that humility is stronger than pride. Hanuman is a role model of self-control, selfless service, and devotion through his love and service to Lord Rama.

Avatars

An avatar is the appearance of a deity on earth in physical form. Vishnu, the sustainer of creation, appears throughout time as needed or when a crisis must be addressed to restore balance. There are ten appearances of Vishnu in this age, nine of which are said to have already taken place. The most well-known avatars of Vishnu include Prince Rama—the hero of the epic poem the Ramayana—and Lord Krishna of the Bhagavad Gita. Vishnu's final avatar is said to be coming at the end of this cycle in the form of a liberator named Kalki. Kalki is sometimes depicted in fierce images as the destroyer of evil forces. (Kalki is not to be confused with Kali, the Hindu goddess of time, motherhood, feminine energy, creativity, and fertility.)

Devas

The devas are the hundreds of gods that make up the Hindu spiritual worldview. There are thirty-three principle devas. Devas personify the forces of nature. For example, Indra, the god of war embodies the energy of storms; Varuna embodies water; and Agni, fire. Devas may also be more abstract, representing ideas such as knowledge or joy, and sometimes as energies that influence life.

I Accept It All as Intended for Me

Whoever with devotion offers Me a leaf, a flower, a fruit, or water, that I accept—the devout gift of the pure-minded. Whatever thou doest, whatever thou eatest, whatever thou offerest in sacrifice, whatever thou givest away, whatever austerity thou practisest, O son of Kunti [Prince Arjuna], do that as an offering unto me. —*Srimad Bhagavad-Gita* 18:26–27[1]

I had lunch recently with the rabbi who performed my wedding ceremony. I am not Jewish, and neither is my spouse. We asked the rabbi, a close friend, to marry us because we couldn't imagine anyone else officiating our marriage. This rabbi has consistently spoken out for the oppressed, stands for social justice, and is an icon of authenticity in our community across faith traditions. If we were Jewish, he'd be our rabbi. At lunch, I was discussing the possibility of teaching a class with him about the spirituality of anger supported by teachings from the Old Testament and New Testament. The rabbi interrupted me with feigned crossness and said, "Edward, there is no Old Testament, there is only *the* Testament." With the gentlest humor, he had pointed out my misconception: the whole world does not share the Christian perspective I had been raised with. To the rabbi, his holy book had not been updated, renewed, or fulfilled by anything. Although we laughed it off, I grew in the awareness that day of how easy it is to misunderstand another culture's ways. The comment lingered in my thoughts. I wondered how many such innocent cultural and spiritual faux pas I had made through ignorance when writing this book. I took my comfort from Lord Krishna's utterances on the importance of sincerity as the factor that makes every kind of offering acceptable to him. I understand that. Innocent sincerity makes forgiveness possible. Innocent sincerity makes it possible even for lighthearted acceptance of errors without the need for indignant correction.

Some twenty-five years ago, a colleague of mine was visiting a predominantly non-Christian country. She went to a large department store to complete some late Christmas shopping and was startled by a bizarre spectacle displayed in the entrance. On the prominently placed Christmas tree in honor of their Western visitors' upcoming holy festival, Santa Claus was attached to a crucifix at the top of the tree. My colleague was horrified for a moment until she saw the smiling faces of the department store staff who were sincerely proud of their bold statement of welcome. My colleague reported that she felt no need to do anything other than have a blessed day shopping in a store that clearly wanted to be inclusive and welcome her.

I wrote this book not as an expert, but as a devotee. I am confident that there is more for me to learn and understand. Still, I continue to be sincerely interested in helping people find access to one of the most beautiful scriptures I have ever read.

And, as a beginner myself, I feel compelled to tell you that there is a whole world of wonder and revelation waiting for you beyond what I have presented in this book.

My own spiritual mentor, Dr. Ernest Holmes, said of the Bhagavad Gita that it was among the most beautiful spiritual works he had read. So much so that he and his brother, Fenwicke Holmes, wrote a tribute to it called *The Song Celestial,* with the same eighteen chapters, four main characters, and similar dialogue between the seeker and the presence of the Divine. I believe I am in the same category as Dr. Holmes and his brother: deeply impressed by the Bhagavad Gita, and as a non-Hindu, trying to integrate its message into my life and worldview without any offense intended.

In the closing chapter of the Bhagavad Gita, Lord Krishna wraps things up by strongly assuring Prince Arjuna that anyone who studies the sacred dialogue between them will have conducted an act of worship to God. He continues, saying that even the person who openheartedly hears the wisdom imparted in their conversation will attain happiness. With that in mind, I urge you now to read the full text of the Bhagavad Gita. I have recommended several versions that are a good place to start for first-time readers, and now that you are equipped with the backstory from the Mahabharata and some knowledge of important Hindu spiritual terms, I am confident that you will experience the same clarity Prince Arjuna described at the end of the Bhagavad Gita when he said his delusions had been destroyed, his memory restored, and his doubts removed.

Acknowledgments

Thank you to the people who supported the creation of this book: William Abel, Emily Edmonds, Dave Edmonds, Christopher Fritzsche, Dr. Ara Gabrielian, Kathy Galvin, and Kevin Viljoen. Thank you for your endurance, corrections, encouragement, and suggestions. Thank you to Joel Fotinos, and the team at St. Martin's Press for guiding me through the completion of the project. I am grateful for the writings of Eknath Easwaran (*The Bhagavad Gita,* and *A More Ardent Fire*) that have inspired and informed my understanding of the Bhagavad Gita and its important message about devotional life.

Appendix: Resources

I have compiled a list of books that in my estimation will make excellent next steps in your reading the Bhagavad Gita. I have also included suggestions for reading the Mahabharata, the Ramayana, and resources for learning about Hinduism in general. My goal is to present books and sources that are easy to read.

Bhagavad Gita

Easwaran, Eknath, trans. *The Bhagavad Gita.* Chapter introductions by Diana Morrison. Tomales, CA: Nilgiri Press, 2009.

> This beautiful and easy-to-read version of the Bhagavad Gita has become my go-to text for clear, concise reference. The chapter introductions are informative and helpful for understanding the content.

Hawley, Jack. *The Bhagavad Gita: A Walkthrough for Westerners.* Novato, CA: New World Library, 2001.

> An easy-to-understand, modern English rendition of the Bhagavad Gita synthesized by the author from thirty versions. The fresh, clear language brings ancient Hindu concepts to life for modern readers.

Mitchell, Stephen, trans. *Bhagavad Gita: A New Translation*. New York: Harmony Books, 2000.

> A beautifully poetic and easy-to-read rendition of the Bhagavad Gita. The introduction and clarity of language throughout make this an excellent read for beginners.

Zaehner, R. C., trans. *The Bhagavad Gita with a Commentary Based on the Original Sources*. London: Oxford University Press, 1973.

> This edition includes a transliteration of the Sanskrit showing the complexity and difficulty of creating an English equivalent of the original text. The commentary is thorough and fascinating.

Gandhi, M. K. *Gandhi for 21st Century: The Teaching of the Gita*. Edited by Anand T. Hingorani. Mumbai: Bhavan's Book University, 1998.

> A collection of writings by Mohandas Gandhi on key teachings from the Bhagavad Gita.

The Mahabharata

Pattanaik, Devdutt. *Jaya: An Illustrated Retelling of the Mahabharata*. New Delhi: Penguin Books, 2010.

> A gorgeous, illustrated, retelling of the Mahabharata with carefully placed commentary so as not to interrupt the flow of the story. It is written in a contemporary style that is enjoyable to read straight through or to pick up anywhere in the story.

Ramayana

Sharma, Bulbul. *The Ramayana for Children*. New Delhi: Puffin Books, 2003.

> This illustrated children's book provides a perfect introduction to the Ramayana for adults who are unfamiliar with the story. It is exciting to read, and K. P. Sudesh's art throughout brings the drama to life on the pages. You might want to begin with this children's version before attempting a complete retelling of the Ramayana.

Egenes, Linda, and Kumuda Reddy. *The Ramayana: A New Retelling of Valmiki's Ancient Epic*. New York: TarcherPerigee, 2016.

> The Ramayana is the other great epic poem of Hinduism. It chronicles the story of Prince Rama, an avatar of Vishnu, in a quest to fulfill his duty to his family, nation, and God. The Ramayana shares many of the same themes as the Mahabharata and is equally respected and loved.

Banker, Ashok K. *Prince of Ayodhya: Book One of the Ramayana*. New York: Warner Books, 2003.

> A dramatization of the story of the Ramayana by one of India's celebrated storytellers, Ashok Banker. This very successful series has been translated into seven languages. It is an exciting and compelling read.

Hinduism

Johnsen, Linda. *The Complete Idiot's Guide to Hinduism*. Indianapolis: Alpha Books/New York: Penguin Random House, 2009.

> Don't let the title fool you: this is an excellent resource and my go-to reference for understanding the big picture of Hinduism. The lighthearted and contemporary writing makes reading about and understanding Hinduism genuinely pleasurable. Linda Johnsen's accessible writing has helped me sort out complicated cultural and spiritual connections more so than almost any other resource.

Cross, Stephen. *The Elements of Hinduism*. Shaftesbury, Dorset: Element Books, 1994.

> An easy-to-read summary of the four essential aspects of Hinduism, its sacred texts, and spiritual cosmology.

Notes

Introduction

1. Jack Hawley, *The Bhagavad-Gita: A Walkthrough for Westerners* (Novato, CA: New World Library, 2001).
2. "Swami Vivekananda at the World Congress of Religions, September 11, 1893," Traditional Yoga and Meditation of the Himalayan Masters, http://www.swamij.com/swami-vivekananda-1893.htm.
3. C. S. Shah, "Vivekananda and Nivedita: Timeless Master and Timely Disciple," *Nectar of Non-Dual Truth* 5 (no. 3), Summer 2004: 18.

What You Should Know About the Bhagavad Gita

1. Swami Prabhavananda and Christopher Isherwood, trans., *The Song of God: Bhagavad-Gita* (New York: Penguin Group, 1972).

Bhagavad Gita's Cast of Characters

1. Eknath Easwaran, trans. *The Bhagavad Gita*, chapter introductions by Diana Morrison (Tomales, CA: Nilgiri Press, 2009).
2. See "The Backstory from the Mahabharata" for an account of Bhishma's heroic sacrifice.

The Bhagavad Gita: A Paraphrase

1. Dharma is one of the central concepts of the Bhagavad Gita and Hinduism. The word *duty* is commonly used as a synonym for *dharma*, and points to conforming to one's personal duty, or character. Even so, the word *duty* is not sufficient to convey everything *dharma* means. See the chapter "Hindu Spiritual Worldview" for a more complete description of dharma.

2. Jnana-yoga, the path of spiritual wisdom.

3. Karma-yoga, the path of selfless service.

4. I have omitted from the paraphrase Lord Krishna's reference in this chapter, verse 13, to the caste system as having its origin in him. Some readers have taken this statement as validation of the caste system in Hindu societies today, while others, such as Hindu priest Vipin Aery, take it to mean that the castes are natural divisions in all human society, created by Lord Krishna but are not based on birth.

5. Vivasvat is one of the names for the Hindu god of the sun, also known as Surya. He is a form of the creator who brings light, life, and warmth to creation and is the originator of humankind.

6. All matter in creation rises from three primary qualities called gunas. These three qualities are challenging to represent with a single English word. The first and highest quality, sattva, is harmony, truth, goodness, balance, joy, and so on. The second, rajas, is passion, energy, and movement. The third, tamas, is the absence of energy, darkness, indifference, and ignorance. Swami Nikhilananda's translation of Chapter fourteen, line twenty of *The Bhagavad Gita* (New York: Ramakrishna-Vivekananda Center, 1944), says that "when the embodied soul has risen above the three gunas of which its body is made, it gains deliverance from birth, death, old age, and pain and becomes immortal" because such a person is no longer at the mercy of their sense perceptions.

7. Brahman is God, or the ultimate reality of all being, not to be confused with Brahma of the trinity. See the chapter "Hindu Spiritual Worldview" for a description of the difference between the two.

8. *Adhyatma* is a combination of two words: *adhi* meaning "over," and *atma* meaning "the self." It is Brahman's nature in all creatures.

9. *Adhibhuta* is the physical world, or perishable matter.

10. *Adhidaiva* is the eternal and all-pervasive spirit

11. Aum, or Om, is an invocation at the beginning and ending of sacred readings or prayer practice. It symbolizes the beginning, continuation, and dissolution of creation. Aum represents the impersonal absolute source of all that is, which is considered to be unknowable. Therefore, a symbol is necessary to represent it: ॐ.

12. Sir Edwin Arnold's 1885 translation of this section in chapter nine is included here for its poetic beauty:

> I am the Sacrifice! I am the Prayer!
> I am the Funeral-Cake set for the dead!
> I am the healing herb! I am the ghee,
> The Mantra, and the flame, and that which burns!
> I am—of all this boundless Universe—
> The Father, Mother, Ancestor, and Guard!
> The end of Learning! That which purifies
> In lustral water! I am OM! I am
> Rig-Veda, Sama-Veda, Yajur-Ved;
> The Way, the Fosterer, the Lord, the Judge,
> The Witness; the Abode, the Refuge-House,
> The Friend, the Fountain and the Sea of Life
> Which sends, and swallows up; Treasure of Worlds
> And Treasure-Chamber! Seed and Seed-Sower,
> Whence endless harvests spring! Sun's heat is mine;
> Heaven's rain is mine to grant or to withhold;
> Death am I, and Immortal Life I am,
> Arjuna! SAT and ASAT, Visible Life,
> And Life Invisible!

Sat is a Sanskrit word meaning the unchangeable reality. *Asat* is the opposite of *sat* and means that which is false or not real.

13. Here the word *soul* is used for *Atman*. The word *soul* is inadequate as an equivalent for *Atman*. See the definition of *Atman* in the chapter "Hindu Spiritual Worldview."

14. In Sanskrit, the title of chapter sixteen is "Divine and Demonic Tendencies." It is an unusually harsh chapter, and somewhat of a departure from the kindhearted language Lord Krishna uses throughout the rest of the Bhagavad Gita. Perhaps the intense language is intended to serve as a wake-up call to the seriousness of following a downward path of succumbing to selfish obsessions. I have attempted to represent this chapter by describing the choice we have to evolve or degrade our spiritual selves. At the end of the chapter, Lord Krishna advises Prince Arjuna to follow the scriptures as the way of avoiding dangerous choices.

The Backstory from the Mahabharata

1. Barbara Stoler Miller, trans., *The Bhagavad-Gita: Krishna's Counsel in Time of War* (New York: Bantam Books, 1986).

2. See the chapter "Hindu Spiritual Worldview" for a definition of dharma.

3. "Mahabharat: Full Animated Movie," in English, https://youtu.be/Xx4H_yuZbmU.

4. Lord Krishna is not only a neighboring prince but a conscious embodiment of God, an avatar of Vishnu: God come to earth in human form to assist in the rebalancing of a world that has become unruly. Vishnu returns to earth in the form of an avatar whenever such a need arises. Another well-known and loved avatar of Vishnu is Lord Rama of the epic poem the Ramayana.

5. Vasus are eight elemental gods: Dharā, god of the Earth; Anala (also called Agni), god of fire; Anila, god of wind; Āpa, god of water; Pratyūṣa, god of the sun; Prabhāsa, god of the sky; Soma, god of the Moon; Dhruva, god of the north star.

6. Veda Vyasa is considered to be both the author of the Mahabharata and a character in it. He is Satyavati's son from her union with the sage

Parashara before she married Shantanu. Veda Vyasa is also the sage who organized the Vedas in four volumes and one of the seven immortals of Hinduism (Chiranjivins).

7. Diwaker Ikshit Srivastava, *Decoding the Metaphor Mahabharata* (Mumbai: Inkstate Books, 2017), 20.

8. See the chapter "Hindu Spiritual Worldview" for a definition of dharma.

A Book of War for Times of Peace

1. Madhava is one of the names for Krishna used in the Bhagavad Gita. Like many of the alternative names used, this name has many possible meanings and cultural references.

2. Edwin Arnold, trans., *The Song Celestial* (Cambridge, UK: John Wilson and Son, 1885).

3. M. K. Gandhi, *Gandhi for 21st Century: The Teaching of the Gita,* ed. Anand T. Hingorani (Mumbai: Bhavan's Book University, 1998).

4. Eknath Easwaran, trans. *The Bhagavad Gita,* chapter introductions by Diana Morrison, (Tomales, CA: Nilgiri Press, 2009).

5. Khudiram Bose was an Indian revolutionary who was executed for his failed attempted to assassinate a judge by bombing.

6. Wendy Doniger, "War and Peace in the Bhagavad Gita," a review of *The Bhagavad Gita: A Biography* by Richard H. Davis, *New York Review of Books,* December 4, 2014, https://www.nybooks.com/articles/2014/12/04/war-and-peace-bhagavad-gita/.

The Path of Devotion—Bhakti Yoga

1. Eknath Easwaran, trans. *The Bhagavad Gita,* chapter introductions by Diana Morrison (Tomales, CA: Nilgiri Press, 2009).

2. The drink that gives the gods immortality. Similar in meaning and origin to the word ambrosia.

3. Catherine Ponder, *Open Your Mind to Prosperity,* rev. ed. (Camarillo, CA: DeVorss & Co., 1984).

4. All quotations are from the New International Version (NIV) © 2011.

5. Yoga is a group of practices that originated in India. The Bhagavad Gita discusses four branches of yoga, of which, bhakti yoga is one. See the chapter "Hindu Spiritual Worldview" for more about yoga.

6. Mohandas Gandhi, *Letters from One: Correspondence (and More) of Leo Tolstoy and Mohandas Gandhi; Including "Letter to a Hindu,"* River Drafting Spirit Series, Book 3 (locs. 367–70), Kindle.

Hindu Spiritual Worldview

1. Stephen Mitchell, trans., *Bhagavad Gita: A New Translation* (New York: Harmony Books, 2000).

2. M. K. Gandhi, *An Autobiography, or the Story of My Experiment with Truth* (Ahmedabad: Navajivan Trust Publishing, 1927), trans. Mahadev Desai.

3. Tony Joseph, "Why Christianity Failed in India," *Outlook,* April 13, 2015, https://www.outlookindia.com/magazine/story/why-christianity-failed-in-india/293895.

I Accept It All as Intended for Me

1. Swami Swarupananda, trans., *Srimad Bhagavad-Gita* (1909; repr., Whitefish, MT: Kessinger Publishing, 2012), Kindle.

About the Author

Jane Epstein

Edward Viljoen (pronounced full-YOON) is the senior minister at the Center for Spiritual Living in Santa Rosa, California, and the author of *Ordinary Goodness: The Surprisingly Effortless Path to Creating a Life of Meaning and Beauty*; *The Power of Meditation: An Ancient Technique to Access your Inner Power*; and coauthor (with Joyce Duffala) of *Seeing Good at Work: 52 Weekly Steps to Transform Your Workplace Experience*.

Edward is passionate about helping other ministers and has served the Ministers Ongoing Education Conference for eighteen years. He trained as an interfaith law enforcement chaplain and served on the board of the Sonoma County Law Enforcement Chaplaincy for nineteen years. Other passions include reading science fiction, cycling to raise funds for HIV/AIDS education and treatment, and leading people on spiritual pilgrimages to places in the world to experience new cultures and new ways of understanding the Divine. He lives in California with his husband, Kevin, and his dog, Cooper.

www.edwardviljoen.org